THE DELAYED BOOK OF LAWS

SATURDAY****SATURDAY

THE FIFTH OF MARCH
<u>YEAR</u>
TWO THOUSAND
AND ELEVEN
<u>TIME</u>
ELEVEN FORTY

THANDI GEORGE

authorHOUSE®

AuthorHouse™
1663 Liberty Drive
Bloomington, IN 47403
www.authorhouse.com
Phone: 1-800-839-8640

First published by AuthorHouse   09/09/2011

ISBN: 978-1-4567-9846-8 (sc)
ISBN: 978-1-4567-9847-5 (ebk)

Printed in the United States of America

This book is printed on acid-free paper.

GIVING THANKS

I give my Gratefulness to GOD for showing Himself to me when I was confused and wanted to find out if it was Him talking to me. He assured me by showing me a huge beam of light; which grew bigger and bigger until it looked as if it has camouflage the world and while I was looking GOD'S image walked pass from the East of the beam to the west. And His image seemed to fill the huge beam of light which looked bigger than Earth.

I give my Obligation to our LORD JESUS CHRIST for writing the book through me and opening the doors; which I did not know they existed and for being a wonderful teacher and also for showing Himself to me when I needed Him.

I give my Promise to do my duty to honour our Holy Mother Mary to fulfil The Seven Spiritual Works of Mercy. Which are [1] Admonish sinners [2] To instruct the uninformed [3] To counsel the doubtful [4] To comfort the sorrowful [5] To be patient with those who are sorrowful [6] To forgive offences [7] To pray for the living and the dead. And I would like to thank our Holy Mother for the warmth she gave me when I was writing my first book and seeing her image on my wall increased my faith.

I would also give my thankfulness to my beautiful daughter for the comfort and patient they gave to me while writing the books and thanks for the love notes which they left on my table.

Thank you to all the people in Cape Town who gave me courage to GOD'S PURPOSE. Some of this people were from the ST Georges Cathedral in ST Georges Mall. And some security guards who talked to me daily and sharing the words of GOD with me and all the strangers who stopped me and prayed for me. And all my friends who believed in me and encouraged me to do GOD'S will.

My reverence goes to Author House for believing in my work. Thank you Chito Numez and Hazel Larosa for being patient with me!

Thanks to the Sisters at Schunsttat Retreat Centre in Constantia Cape Town South Africa for looking after me. And for confirming that my spiritual teacher was a part of the Schunstatt Retreat before she left this world.

<u>MAY THE LOVE OF GOD BE WITH ALL OF YOU</u>

ACKNOWLEDGEMENT

THIS BOOK IS DIVIDED IN SEVEN PARTS

[1] PART ONE = INTRODUCTION.

[2] PART TWO = LEARNING TO LIVE A RIGHTEOUS LIFE.

[3] PART THREE = LEARNING THE LAWS OF DEVOTION.

[4] PART FOUR = LEARNING HOW TO OVERCOME EVIL DEEDS AND INCLUDES THE FOUR STAGES OF THE END OF THE TIME.

[5] PART FIVE = LEARNIG TO RECOGNISE THE SINGS OF THE END AND IT INCLUDES THE DELAYED BOOK OF MESSAGES.

[6] PART SIX = LEARNING TO RECOGNISE THE SIGNS OF THE END AND INCLUDES THE LAWS WE HAVE TO KEEP.

[7] PART SEVEN = UPDATE OF NEW MESSAGES= AND EXPLAINS THE RAPTURE WHICH WAS TO TAKE PLACE IN MAY IN THE YEAR TWO THOUSAND AND ELEVEN, IT ALSO EXPLAINS THE DIFFERENCE BETWEEN RAPTURE ANDRUPTURE.

PLEASE READ AND ENJOY TRAVELLING THIS JOURNEY WITH US!

PART ONE = [1]

INTRODUCTION

Today the weather is very hot in the city of Cape Town in South Africa. I am strolling around the City feeling very happy I have now reached the St Georges Mall, watching all the entertainers wiggling their bodies gracefully.

I see a man carrying something on his head which looks very heavy and decorated with all sorts of things including egg shells and he is carrying a homemade cell-phone on his hand which is made from a cardboard. And he is pretending to be talking to someone.

Everyone is looking at this man and they are all amused by his actions, and now he tries to encourage someone to do the same and the person runs away because they think the man is out of his mind.

Then I looked carefully at this amazing man. That is when I realise that he is also one of the entertainers. So I carried on walking, I came across a group of people who were giving out leaflets.

I took a leaflet and read it. But, to my surprise, the leaflet was talking about the end of the world which will take place this year twenty eleven on the tenth of October [10/10/2011].

WELL!—I thought; what am I going to do now because I have been writing the book about our Spiritual Journey and the book is almost ready to be published, all I need is to get a publisher.

I have tried hard to look for a publisher in South Africa but it is difficult because I need a lot of money to pay for the publishing, so I thought; what I need to do will be to sell my car to raise money to pay for publishing.

Because the book which I have written it is automatically written through me by our LORD who asked me in the year two thousand and six [2006] to work for the Him, and write about the messages which He wants the world to know about what will take place in the future.

I will start with the message which makes me wonder about the truth of the end of the world, as we all know that there has been so many predictions which are still puzzling our minds and making us constantly wondering about what we should do and what not to do.

One of the messages which I received from the LORD was that it is true that the world is coming to the end. And that we should all start preparing ourselves for His coming and the LORD also mentioned the messenger who will come before Him to come and prepare us.

It was now in the year two thousand and eight when the LORD showed me the new born baby who was born on the thirtieth of December in the year two thousand and eight [30/12/2008. And the LORD told me that this baby is the reincarnation of king Josiah who was a good servant of GOD, and now GOD is bringing him back to the world, he is the one who will come before the LORD.

KING JOSIAH

The LORD did tell me that it is true that the world is coming to the end. He also confirmed that there will be a messenger who will come before him to prepare us. the LORD also showed me the baby who was born in the year two thousand and eight [30/12/2008] and told me that this baby is the spirit of Josiah and this spirit has taken a knew body and a new name. And he is the one who will come and prepare us and teach us and confirm what is written in the Bible and he will teach us about the laws which we should keep to, to be able to reach the Kingdom of Heaven.

The LORD said Josiah will only show his Gift at the age of fifteen [15years old] which will be the year two thousand and twenty three [2023] and he will be with us for only two years [two years] which means he will be seventeen years old when he dies and that will be the year two thousand and twenty five [2025]. Then the LORD will come and collect all the good people who are still in the world and this will be the time of the end of the world.

THE YEAR 2025

This gives us the year two thousand and twenty five [2025] to be the end of the world because; if Josiah was born in the year 2008 and he will be fifteen years when he starts preparing us, and he will be with us for only two years. That gives us the year two thousand and twenty five [2025]. But I was not sure about the day or month when this will happen.

THIS is how I worked the end to be in the year 2025. I took the date of birth which is the year 2008 plus the 15years when he starts to fulfil his purpose, which gave me the year 2023 plus the two years [2years] which he will be preparing us, and that gives me the year 2025.

The amazing thing is:—while I was writing all this down, I received a message from the LORD telling me to look at the photo of the mystery of my clock which started going anti-clockwise in the year two thousand and six [2006]. And the LORD said to me I will find the day and the month and the year when the end will take place.

I stood up to find the photo of my clock which was in the front page of our local newspaper in the year two thousand and six, talking about the mystery of my clock. When I looked at the clock to see what the LORD has instructed me to do.

The voice of the LORD said to me if I look carefully on the picture of the clock in the newspaper, I will see that the time on the clock which went anti-clockwise which is the [crystal clock] on the left of the picture says the time is ten minutes past seven and that will give me the numbers seven and ten 7-10 and when I look at the clock which is next to the clock which is going anti-clockwise. I will notice that the time on that clock says the time is nearly ten twenty five [10/25] and the ticking of the seconds is on seven [7]. While I was puzzled about what the LORD is telling me, that is when the voice of the LORD said to me Take the seven and write it in front of the number ten, and then twenty five and that will give me the day and the month and the year of the end of the world. Then the LORD said to me the number seven always means the completion and the number ten always means the beginning and the end.

So I followed the instruction given by the LORD, and this is what came out:—[7/10/25]. I must admit I was very surprise to learn the ways of the LORD, I felt peace and joy after the LORD has spoken to me. Then I learned that I must work hard and finish writing the messages which the LORD has asked me to write. So that we can all get ready for His coming.

I am still puzzled with this photo because when I noticed the clock going anti-clockwise in the year two thousand and six [2006] I thought it was funny and never given a thought that one day the LORD will explain to me that my clock was actually talking to us and giving us the date of the end of time. And the LORD is confirming this mystery to me in the year two thousand and ten [2010] four years after the mystery has occurred. It is true that the LORD works miraculously.

Another thing which confused me was when the LORD said to me that when I look at the clock which its time was moving clockwise when He said the time was <u>nearly</u> twenty five minutes past ten. I would have thought the LORD would have said to me the time was twenty two minutes past ten but when I questioned the LORD, He told me that yes it is <u>nearly</u> the end of time and this is why He says the time is nearly twenty five minutes past ten. And the LORD also reminded me that <u>ten means the Beginning</u>

and the End and if I take the zero from the ten I will be left with one which means the beginning and if I put back the zero that gives me ten which means the END. Then the LORD carried on to say to me the twenty five minutes on the clock means the end of the world and while I was still confused, then He carried on to—say if I write the number twenty five down I will notice that it has two digits which are two and five [25] and then separate them and put a plus sign in between and add them together that will give me a seven number [2+5=7] which will bring me back to the seven number which means the END.

I hope you enjoyed the teachings of the LORD! Pease enjoy your spiritual journey. Please believe me the LORD is a wonderful teacher who is full of love.

THE PICTURE

OF

THE MYSTERY CLOCK

THAT'S ME ON THIS PICTURE—DON'T I LOOK SURPRISED?

PLEASE NOTE

Please look carefully at the picture and you will see that the LORD is the one who did this mystery to warn us and to confirm the end.

When we look carefully at the story of King Josiah we will realise that the confirmation on King Josiah also confirms the year 2025 to be the end of time.

When we also look again at the clock which its hand ticking was moving anti-clockwise also gives us the numbers which are 7/10 but does not give the third number because the hand ticking when the photo was taken it was on top of the minute hand of the clock.

After writing all this down, then I decided to read the leaflet which I was given at the St George Mall again to compare the dates which were predicted. I found out that there was a huge gap between the dates I was given and the dates on the leaflet.

So I decided that I will carry on writing the messages which I have received from the LORD. The main important thing is to do what I am told to do and also to start preparing myself.

I decided to re-look again for the third time at the leaflet which I was given while I was strolling around the Market Squire in Cape Town South Africa, which was warning us about the end of time on the 10/10/2011 and started to compare my dates and theirs again. My dates still confirmed the end of the world to be on the 7/10/2025.

I came to the conclusion that whatever year the world comes to the end it will be fine for me and those who are ready, because we all can see the signs of the end, but some people prefer not to think about it and some do not want to believe in the end.

I myself believe that there is no harm not believing what other people believe. The most important thing is to learn and understand that GOD has sent these messages through the prophets from the beginning and GOD has also sent his son

JESUS CHRIST to confirm all what will take place in the future, and now GOD is sending messages through the chosen people who live amongst us to be HIS messengers.

The duty of the messenger of GOD is to do what he is told to do, and the messenger of GOD will act according to the instructions which he is given. All we can do is to prepare ourselves, by living according to the teachings of our LORD, and teachings of all the good prophets of the past and prophets of today.

I myself believe in fulfilling GOD'S will, because I want to see GOD. As GOD has always been a mystery to all of us. So, I see no point of working hard and doing all good things to the world and not being able to see our mystery Father, whom the prophets have been talking about and our LORD JESUS CHRIST has confirm, that, He comes from the Father. And; also whatever the Bible says and other Religions teaches us that there is a higher being which controls our lives.

My spirit is longing to reach its higher purpose and my body is getting tired of the pain it endures in this world.

I have also learned that whatever we do on earth we will leave it on earth when we die, because it belongs to earth, and all I want now is my spirit to go back where it came from. There is one thing I did not really understand in my life. Is when people continually fighting each other for the land and also the wars which are constantly going on from the beginning of the world until now. This whole process disturbed me completely and made me wonder why are some people doing all these killing just for the Land which they can't take with them when they die?

It was when I received the message from the LORD after I have questioned Him about the disasters which are taking place in the world when He told me that everything is meant to be and it will stay that way until the end of the world and all these disasters are mainly for our spiritual growth. The LORD also explained to me that Earth was created for our life lessons.

I have also asked GOD to show himself to me so that I can be able to believe that the messages which I am receiving are true messages from GOD and He did show Himself to me. And GOD also showed Himself to me about three times since I started to receive messages.

Please read all about our Spiritual gifts and our Spiritual journey in the book of messages which I have written which is called; LET US CELEBRATE THE END OF TIME AND DANCE TO THE MUSIC OF TIME.

It is true that our Creator is with us always and he knows us better than we know ourselves.

THE other thing I found very interesting is that the leaflet which I have received, had a lot of work gone through it. And the calculations and the quoting of the scripture is convincing.

THE SEVEN THOUSAND YEARS [7,000]

AND

THE FOUR THOUSAND AND NINE HUNDRED AND NINETY

YEARS [4,990]

AS one of the messages which the leaflet points out, is the message which, says:—Years ago we learned from the Bible that the flood occurred in the year 4,990 B.C. More recently we learned that judgement day is to occur in the year 2011 A.D. The year 2011 is exactly 7,000 years after the year 4,990 B.C.

I found these calculations very interesting. Because in one of the messages I have received was that now we are nearly reaching the seven thousand years [7,000] when we will become one nation. At the time when I received this message it was when GOD was preparing me to work for him, and I did not understand what GOD was saying to me.

TRANSFORMATION

I can remember telling my daughter that I have received a message that we are all going to become one nation. But; I did not understand this message clearly. So I decided not to bother about it and not even to mention this in the books I have written. Now I am very happy to learn that my message is true and now I also understand that the message actually confirms what the Bible said. It said:—We will all be transformed.

1 CORINTHIANS 50-54

Apostle Paul says:—I declare to you, brothers, that flesh and blood cannot inherit the Kingdom of GOD nor does the perishable inherit the imperishable.

Listen, I tell you the mystery: We will not all sleep, but we will all be changed—in a flash, in the twinkling of an eye, at the last trumpet.

For the trumpet will sound, the dead will be raised imperishable, and we will be changed for the perishable must clothe itself with the imperishable, and the mortal with immortality.

When the perishable has been clothed with the imperishable and the mortal with immortality, then the saying that is written will come true:

Death has been swallowed up in victory.

WHERE OR DEATH IS YOUR VICTORY

WHERE OR DEATH IS YOUR STRING

Now: as I continue to look at the leaflet again to try and match some of the messages which I have received. I came across this paragraph which reads:—Our salvation is entirely completed at the time the true believers receive their eternally alive, resurrected bodies. This is what happens on the day of Rapture, May 21/2011. Thus the period from 1 April 33 A.D. to May 21/2011 [inclusive] is the complete period from the time GOD shows us how our salvation was accomplished to the time our salvation has been entirely completed.

THIS coincides perfectly with the number ten, which signifies completeness.

I also received a similar message but, my dates are for the year 2012 and I call the year 2012 the year of celebration for all the spirits who are still in earthly body and the spirits who have discarded their bodies ready to incarnate back to earth to finish the lessons which they need to complete, all these spirits will be celebrating their fifth level of their spiritual growth, this spirits will be anointed by our LORD JESUS CHRIST to be the chosen ones, it is called a spiritual shifting from one level to the next.

THIS shifting is very important to all of us and our LORD is very pleased with these spirits because they have done well, and the LORD is very happy because since the beginning of creation which was the beginning of our life lessons this is a highest percentage of the spirits which are moving from the fourth level to the fifth level and it is sixty nine percentage [69%] of the whole world popualtion which have achieved this shifting which is really great.

The year two thousand and twelve [2012]:—it is the celebration of these spirits who are still around us and the spirits who have left this world. Everyone who will be one of these people who will be celebrating in the year twenty twelve they will receive spiritual messages which will be send to them through messages from strangers or people around them even children will prophesy, even, through dreams or visions or they will come across people who will start talking to them about seeing the light of GOD through them. Some people may even want to pray and bless these people because GOD our Father is going to work through all of us. The spirits who have left this world and are waiting to incarnate, they will celebrate in spirit in the Spiritual Planet where they are waiting at this moment of time.

We can never enter Heaven before the end of time, now this is the time when our LORD JESUS CHRIST is coming to fulfil what He already told us that He will come again and award each of us according to our deeds, and then He will take all the anointed ones with Him. The LORD has already started anointing His chosen ones and He is still carrying on with His duty. People who have left this world they are not in Heaven they have been reincarnating to be able to finish the lessons of life. The doors of Heaven are not yet opened they can be only opened at the end of time by our LORD JESUS CHRIST as He promised.

Do not worry, because there is still time to change, but changes must be made soon. And please if you have been going through a difficult time, you were only being tested, do not give up your faith, keep on praying because you are one of the chosen ones and GOD our Father is looking after you. What is happening is that you are also being transformed, you are only discarding the earthly body and you are receiving a spiritual body.

IT is time for the Holy Bible to fulfil its purpose, we must all rejoice, because; this is the time we were all waiting for; For a long time since we came to earth to learn the lessons of life, now our learning is over. Those who will graduate they will and those who will hold their spiritual Masters Degrees they will and those who will be honoured in different ways they will.

Only our LORD JESUS can be a judge and no one else. So let's get ready and change our ways, because it is very exciting to see the LORD opening the Gates of Heaven. Please do not doubt there is Heaven as there is Earth.

Earth is our School

Heaven is our Home

We are spirits which have taken a body only for the purpose of our life lesson. This is why every life we took out of our thousand lives we managed to take a different body, so that we can be able to learn that lesson which GOD our Father has written in our book of life to learn.

Those who are not Celebrating in the year two thousand and twelve [2012] they are reaching other levels of their spiritual growth, and their time will come. Some have already celebrated their levels.

The percentage of people [Spirits] who have reached their seven level of their spiritual growth is twenty per-cent [20%] out of the whole world population, which is the highest level which we need to achieve. Some of this spirits are among us and some of these spirits are waiting for the end of time in the Spiritual Planet and still fulfilling GOD'S purpose.

This message I received from our LORD JESUS when He was teaching me about our seven levels of our Spiritual growth and teaching me how we achieved these levels by using diagrams which explained clearly about reincarnation and our thousand years which GOD gave each individual to learn their life lessons.

IT is true what I have read from the leaflet though my dates and their dates do not match. What is important is the message itself which seems to coincide with each other.

I believe; it is true that we are reaching the end. The sins are visible all we need to do is to keep to THE TEN COMMANDMENTS OR ANY OTHER TEACHINGS OF THE PROPHETS OF GOD. Whatever Religion you are; please pick what is good teaching and discard the bad. That's all we need to do. We cannot criticise any more we were all learning the lessons of life. No Religion is better than another

JAMES 4: 14

BOASTING ABOUT TOMORROW

Now listen, you who say, today or tomorrow we will go to this or that City, spend a year there carry on the business and make money. Why? You don not even know what will happen tomorrow.

What is your life?

You are a mist that appears for a little while

AND

Then vanishes

Instead you ought to say:—If it is the LORD'S will let it be!

* * *

I am happy that my walk on the fifth of March twenty eleven [5/3/2011] which I took at:—eleven forty in ST Georges Mall Cape Town became fruitful and courageous. This is why I decided to sit and write this book of messages, which, the LORD once asked me to write in the year 2007, and I did not have time to write it, because I was still writing the book called:—TALKING POETRY. I guise this book is what our LORD wants me to finish writing, because our time is limited.

I WILL DO GOD'S WILL NOT MY WILL.

THIS IS THE

MESSAGE FROM THE LORD JESUS CHRIST

IT was in the beginning of the year two thousand and five [2005] when I wrote my first book of messages when the LORD JESUS told me that I must write the book of laws which will help us to change our ways of life, because now we have reached the end of our lessons in life and it is time to look back at the teachings of Moses and the commands which we have to keep.

PLEASE NOTE

The most important thing about this message is that everything we have gone through in the world, however evil or good; it will always be the same in generations to come because it is meant to be for our spiritual growth. Whether pain or happiness, sickness or health, birth and death they are all part of our spiritual growth. Even wars and good behaviour or bad behaviour is meant to be for our spiritual growth. As it was in the beginning will be the same at the end. This routine goes on until the end of our life lessons on earth. Unfortunately; the end of our-lessons on earth are almost over in this world, and this is why it is the time to discard all evil deeds.

This is why the LORD has asked me to remind everyone from all corners of the world and whatever religion you may worship to discard all evil deeds and start serving each individuals with love. Because this is the time when Religion has fulfilled its purpose, now it is for each individual to find their own truth about serving humanity with love as each one is accountable for their own spiritual growth there is no time to be instructed by others to practice evil deeds anymore, because now we are reaching the end of time and individuals will be judged separately. There;—is no more excuses that we do not know right or wrong because we have been incarnating since the beginning of time. And through our incarnate we have learned all the lessons of life by discarding one body and taking another for specific lessons. During the incarnation we have chosen different gender, colour, country and religion for the purpose of our life lessons. This is why we are taught not to judge anyone.

Nothing comes to the end.

But!

Everything changes form.

This is why we call the <u>End of the world</u> the <u>End of time.</u>

PART TWO

LEARNING TO LIVE A RIGHTEOUS LIFE

WE WILL START BY LEARNING SOME OF THE READINGS FROM THE BIBLE SO THAT WE CAN REFRESH OURSELVES AS THE LORD ASKED ME TO QOUTE THESE FOLLOWING TEACHINGS WHCH WILL HELP US TO DISCARD EVIL DEEDS.

The following quoting's from the bible were chosen by the LORD Himself and these teachings are for all Religions to learn—as the LORD JESUS CHRIST is the one to open the doors of Heaven for all of us and He is the one who will come and choose the good people out of this world to heaven.

All the prophets of the past were chosen to come and teach the ways of GOD who is one GOD to all and the prophets of today are here to remind us about the teachings of the prophets of the past. And this is why this book is written so that it can remind us about the end of our lessons.

LET US LEARN ABOUT WHAT THE BIBLE TEACHES US;

ABOUT

WHICH GOOD DEEDS WE HAVE TO PRACTICE!

AND

HOW TO AVOID PRACTISING EVIL DEED!

1 CORINTHIANS 15: 33

Bad company corrupts good character; Come back to your senses as you ought!

AND

Stop sinning; for there are some who are ignorant of GOD!

WHY

Do we seek the answer to the End? When; we haven't yet found the answers from the beginning.

LET US LEARN THE WORDS OF WISDOM

WORDS OF WISDOM

Words of wisdom will teach us to understand Nature and to live in Harmony with all GOD'S creation. So that we can achieve the comfort of health and progress, both:—Spiritual and Physical. And help us to become one with nature and once we become one with nature that will help us to become a part of nature.

WHEN

We become one with nature, we gain Humanity

AND

Once we have gained humanity

We will not fear that someone will overlook us.

We will learn that we are one with each other.

AND

We will stay one with each other till the end.

Staying one with each other is very important to us; as we are all part of each other, because we have one Father who is GOD and

He is a part of us which—His light shines through us when we serve each other with love.

PSALMS 27-1

THE LORD is my light and salvation—Whom shall I fear?

THE LORD is my stronghold—Whom shall I fear?

GOD PROVIDES AND GOD GUIDES US

GOD has promised us that whatever we ask for, it will be given to us. So we must not forget the promises of GOD to us because GOD is love He has told us that if we ask we shall receive and if we seek we shall find and if we knock the doors will be opened for us.

ASK, SEEK. AND KNOCK

MATHEW 7:7

Ask, and it will be given to you.

Seek, and you will find.

Knock and the door will be open to you.

Please do not give up on the LORD, no matter
what you are going through.

PATIENCE IN SUFFERING

JAMES 5: 7-19

Be patient, then, brothers, until the LORD'S coming. See how the Famer waits for the land to yield its valuable crop, and how patient he is for the autumn and spring rains. You too, be patient and stand firm, because the LORD's coming is near.

PLEASE TAKE NOT

Life needs patients—there is no easy come nothing comes easy. We all have to work hard to achieve our goals. And with faith in GOD we will reach our goals. If we are not patient this is when evil starts to take over our lives, and the devil starts directing us and teach us how to achieve our goals without having to wait for the right time. And once we have been overcome by evil deeds, that is; when we lose the road to our destiny.

ROMANS 12-21

Do not be overcome by evil; but overcome evil with good.

It is true that we should not honour the World for our GOD or else IT takes us for Its Slave. Only GOD our creator understands His creation and has control over all. And we must not forget what our LORD JESUS CHRIST taught us that everything stays the same it only changes form. And only GOD OUR FATHER can change His creation.

EVERYTHING STAYS THE SAME

BUT

NOW AND AGAIN IT CHANGES FORM

We have seen what the world does to good people as well as bad people, and we have learned that the world is not an easy place to be, for both; rich or poor. Both will feel pain and happiness now and again. We also learned that, nothing much has changed since the beginning of creation, and I can assure you that nothing much will change. When we look at what we think has changed to our eyes, the same thing is being experienced in someone's eyes; it has only changed form.

For example:—What I mean, about changing form:—I mean that when physical abuse is being recognised the perpetrator will use mental abuse to his victim. So that the victim will be unable to show their scars, this is what we see in our daily lives, and we do not know what to do, the powerful become more powerful. The victim stays a victim, generation after generation.

So everything stays the same. And the world will never be a perfect world. We are all here to learn the lessons of life, so we can reach our highest. To reach our Highest all we have to do is to be blameless and live perfect lives.

Those who want to live their evil ways is their choice BUT, the day will come when they will realise that time is limited and they have not turn against their evil ways. I am afraid that it will be too late for them to change.

We must not fear these evil people, because they cannot hurt our spirit they can only hurt the body and delay their spiritual growth. Because the spirit comes from GOD OUR FATHER and the body only houses the spirit. So this is why we should not do evil to each other, because no one can understand the ways of GOD.

<u>LET US LEARN ABOUT THE LOVE OF MONEY</u>

<u>1 THIMOTHY 6: 3-10</u>

If anyone teaches false doctrines and does not agree to the sound instruction of our LORD JESUS CHRIST and to godly teaching, he is conceited and understands nothing.

He has an unhealthy interest in controversies and quarrels about words that result in envy, strife, malicious talk, evil suspicions and constant friction between men of corrupt mind, who have been robbed of the truth and who think that godliness is a means to financial gain.

But, godliness with contentment is great gain. For we brought nothing into the world, and we can take nothing out of it!

But, if we have food and clothing, we will be content with that.

People who want to get rich fall into temptation and a trap and into many foolish and harmful desires that plunge men into ruin and destruction.

For the love of money is a root of all kinds of evil.

Some people, eager for the money, have wondered from the faith and pierced themselves with many grieves.

PLEASE TAKE NOTE

We all know that all kinds of evil are being caused by the love of money. How! can we be controlled by the things of the world when we all know that we cannot take them to the grave with us?

Those who are good must keep on doing their good work, because they are perfect beings of which we all ought to be.

May the love of GOD be with you always and do not give up your good work.

FOR THOSE WHO LOVE GOD

1 THIMOTY 6: 11-16

But you, man of GOD, flee from all this, and pursue righteousness, godliness, faith, love, endurance and gentleness. Fight the good fight of the faith. Take hold of the eternal life to which you were called, when you made your good confession in the presence of many witnesses. In the sight of GOD, who gives life to everything, and of CHRIST JESUS, who while testifying to Pontius Pilate made the good confession!

I charge you to keep this command without spot or blame until the appearing of our LORD JESUS CHRIST, which GOD will bring about in his own time.

GOD the blessed and only ruler, the KING of KINGS and LORD of LORD'S, who alone is immortal and who lives in unapproachable light, whom no—one can see.

TO HIM BE HONOUR AND MIGHT

FOR EVER

AMEN

DOMINION AND AWE BELONGS TO GOD; HE HAS ESTABLISHED ORDER IN THE HIGHEST.

PLEASE TAKE NOTE

WE have all seen human weaknesses on earth and the pain it caused amongst all of us, whether rich or poor because of failing to understand the ways of GOD and failing to believe in the teaching of Religion.

THE teaching of Religion is the only way we can find our way back to GOD our Father. I do understand that some people are angry with religion because of some of the teacher's behaviour.

THAT is not for us to judge because the one who sins is the one who will be accountable for his sins.

THERE is no harm to us, going to the book shops and start reading different religious books and start learning about what other religions are teaching because they all teach about the same GOD who is our Creator even though he Has been given different names by different cultures He is still the same GOD.

NOW it is time for us to search for the meaning of life than being changed by individuals who have lost the meaning of life.

WE must not worry about what our leaders will do for us and what our Priest will do for us; they are just people like us searching for the meaning of life. They are also confused like us. So! We as individuals should search for the meaning of life which is our spiritual journey.

THE leaders are only here to keep control of the country they were chosen to take charge and rule according to the teaching of GOD and not to put border gates so that we cannot be able to know each other and be able to learn from each other and also be able to share our spiritual gifts with each other, and by doing that. They delayed our spiritual journey and they confused us from understanding our lessons of life.

THIS is what caused Discrimination, Hatred and Racism in the World and greed. Not forgetting oppression which has become our daily bread. **THIS** is the **BIGGEST**, mistake which was done to destroy humanity and that spoiled all GOD'S purpose. BUT, keep in mind;—the Leaders at that time they thought they were helping the people and they believed that they were doing the right thing even though they realised that people of GOD were suffering, they still oppressed those they felt like oppressing, and overpowered those they felt they can overpower. But the leaders of today cannot tell us that they do not know what is wrong and what is right.

THAT is when things didn't work according to GOD'S teaching as man has taken charge and ruined it all. So man lost his purpose.

NOW that it is coming to the end, it is time for each individual to search for the real meaning of life because there; is still time to change even though our time is limited on earth we can still change our ways right now at this minute and our sins will be forgiven as the LORD said we were only learning the lessons of life and He promised us that when we turn and ask for forgiveness we will be forgiven.

Mistakes have been made, and there is no time to worry and get angry about the past. And there is no harm looking and learning from the past.

THE world has gone beyond repair and there is nothing we can do about it because it was fulfilling its purpose and now it is exhausted and we are also exhausted and our spirit is now longing for our Father. All we are left with is to be able to forgive each other so that we can be able to move on.

Learning to forgive is a Wonderful Spiritual gift which was received by—President Nelson Mandela of South Africa and the best of all; is that he shared this wonderful gift of forgiveness with the world.

If we find it difficult to forgive we must turn back and learn the teachings of religion and this will also increase our faith in GOD.

FORGIVENESS
IS
WHAT WE ARE LEFT WITH

THE CHURCH and some priest we heard about in the newspapers, about their bad behaviour does not help our spiritual growth at all. **BUT!**—It does not mean that we should stop learning about GOD, because we are all here to learn the lessons of life and we must still keep going to our worshipping places so that we can learn more about GOD. Do not be so angry with what you hear about what goes on in the worshiping places. GOD will see to those evil people. All we need to do is to go in the worshipping places and start learning about GOD, and learn about the good teachings from the teachers of religion and build ourselves to be as solid as a rock and you will not shirk.

THERE are still a lot of Priests all over the world and from all Religions who do not believe in Evil deeds.

PLEASE DO NOT BE PUT OF BY WHAT YOU HEAR EVERYONE IS LEARNING THE LESSONS OF LIFE TO BE ABLE TO REACH THE HIGHER PURPOSE.

THAT means all what we are going through in this life and what we went through in our past lives we were all learning the lessons of life, and what has taken place was meant to take place. It was what it was meant to be, and can never be changed, because only GOD sets the time for everything. <u>SO THAT THE SCRIPTURES CAN BE FULFILED</u>

THE bible tells us about all things which will take place in the world before the end comes. And we can now see the truth but we are running away from the truth because we are frightened of ourselves. All we need to do is to start preparing ourselves for the coming of the LORD. And we must not be afraid of our new image.

DO NOT BE AFRAID

IT is true that; all of us have sinned because we were all learning the lessons of life, and now it is time to change and GOD is ready to forgive us. Our lessons have now come to the end, and we are ready for judgement.

THE Planet Earth has fulfilled its purpose and it now
exhausted.

THE Prophets of the past have fulfilled their purpose.

THE LORD JESUS CHRIST has fulfilled his purpose.

And

He is about to fulfil His promises.

THE BIBLE has now fulfilled its purpose. It started with the book of GENESIS and now we are on the REVELATIONS.

THE DEVIL has now fulfilled his purpose, WHICH WAS TO TEST ALL OF US GOOD OR BAD, RICH OR POOR. He was released only for a short time. Now he has been locked up. But, all who have been touched by the devil. The testing will still go on until we recognise evil and discard it.

THIS is why the world is upside down. We are all being tested our lessons of life are over. EACH will be accountable for their deeds. Because:—you are traveling a journey of self.

PLEASE TAKE NOTE

The LORD told me that we are all being tested and after the testing He will send his counsellor who will prepare us for His coming. Whatever pain you are going through at this moment you are being tested. And please be strong and learn to forgive so that you can be able to move on to another level of your spiritual growth once you have forgiven you do not need to be with the same person but at the end of the day it is your choice whether you want to be friends with the person you have forgiven. DON'T FORGET:—being with the person who once hurt your feelings you will have to learn the Lesson of Trust: which may delay your spiritual growth.

THE DEVIL WAS RELEASED TO COME AND TEST US IN THE YEAR TWO THOUSAND AND FIVE [2005] AND WAS CAGED IN THE YEAR—BECAUSE NOW WE ARE REACHING THE END OF TIME AND WE HAVE USED UP ALL OUR LIVES WHICH GOD GAVE TO US THROUGH REINCARNATION. THERE IS NO TIME TO HANG AROUND WITH EVIL DOERS. START; HANGING AROUND WITH THE GOOD PEOPLE BECAUSE WERE GIVEN A THOUSAND LIVES TO LEARN THE LESSONS OF LIFE AND TO FULFILL OUR PURPOSE OF SERVING ALL GOD'S CREATION WITH LOVE.

REVELATIONS 20: 7-8

WHEN the thousand years are over, Satan will be released from his prison and will go out to deceive the nations in the four corners of the world GOG and MAGOG to gather them for battle.

PLEASE NOTE: *** IN ONE OF THE MESSAGES I RECEIVED FROM THE LORD WAS:—THE DEVIL WAS RELEASED ON THE THIRTYFIRST OF DECEMBER IN THE YEAR TWO THOUSAND AND FIVE [31/12/2005] This why there is so much evil going on in the world because the devil has taken over the world for a few years and then after he will be caged but his evil ways will still roam the world testing those who are still to be tested and when he gets caged, then GOD himself will start taking over the ruling of the world removing all the evil leaders from different countries and cleansing the world from sin before our LORD JESUS CHRIST comes to collect all the remaining good people who are still in the world.

The message you have just read was given to me by the LORD so that I can tell the people all over the world that they must not fear when they see the evil which is going around the world and mass-deaths of humans which will transpire the future of the world it is only the confirmation of the end of time. All we need to do is to love and care for each other.

LOVING EACH OTHER

WE ARE MADE TO LOVE AND CARE FOR EACH OTHER:—THIS IS WHAT THE PRPHETS OF THE PAST AND THE PROPHETS OF TODAY ARE TEACHING US! AND OUR LORD JESUS CHRIST HAS TOLD US TO DO.

JOHN 15: 9-17

OUR LORD JESUS SAYS;—As the Father has loved me, so have I loved you. Now remain in my love. If you obey my commands you will remain in my love, just as I have obeyed my Father's commands and remain in his love. I have told you this so that my joy may be in you and that your joy may be complete.

My command is this: **Love each other as I have loved you**. Greater love has no—one than this that He lay down His love for His friends. You are my friends if you do what I command. I no longer call you servants, because a servant does not know his master's business. Instead, I have called you friends, for everything that I have learned from my Father I have made known to you. You did not choose me, but I chose you and appointed you to go and bear fruit, fruit that will last.

Then the Father will give you whatever you ask in my name. This is my command **LOVE EACH OTHER**.

PLEASE TAKE NOTE

To be able to love is by understanding the ways of GOD and to be able to embrace the love of GOD is to be in meditation.

IN SILENCE

In Silence we learn to hear the voice of GOD

AND

To hear ourselves

AND

To be able to understand Life purpose!

AND

When we understand our life purpose, we will be able to love all GOD'S CREATION.

Because:—love is the noblest frailty of the mind.

When we love we will be able to forgive because forgiveness is the light that leads to freedom.

We must all ask for forgiveness before judgement day.

We must not put of by pride when it is time to ask for forgiveness because pride will only delay our spiritual growth.

A MESSAGE FOR THOSE WHO SHOW PRIDE

GOD opposes the proud

BUT

Gives Grace to the humble

Cast away the pride and become humble, so that our LORD can be able to work through you. You have earned the world now your spirit is ready to earn Heaven. Even the young have come to the end of their life lessons because they have all used up their thousand lives which GOD has given them. They must also take their pride away and start asking for forgiveness so that when the LORD comes they will be ready to receive HIM with delight.

ECCELESIASTES 11: 7-8

REMEMBER YOUR CREATOR WHILR YOUNG

Light is sweet, and it pleases the eyes to see the sun.

However many years a man may live.

Let him enjoy them all.

BUT

Let him remember the day of darkness, for they will be many.

These are the wonderful words from the book of ECCLESAIASTES which we have to keep in mind because they will remind us that pride and jealousy does not work. Both are for the love of world not the love of our Creator as GOD wants us to humble ourselves so that we can be able to reach Him.

PLEASE NOTE

We have learned that the love of <u>THE WORLD</u> and of the next cannot agree in a believer's heart as Fire and Water cannot agree in a single vessel.

<u>LET US BE REAL AND ENTER THROUGH THE RIGHT GATE!</u>

You may be wondering what way is the RIGHT GATE. "Well" the HOLY BIBLE and other Religious Books teaches us that the right GATE is the narrow gate, which needs us to humble ourselves to be able to find the right path which will lead us to the narrow gate.

<u>MATHEW 7:13-14</u>

THE NARROW AND WIDE GATES

Enter through the narrow gate. For wide is the gate and broad is the road that leads to destruction, and many enter through it.

BUT!

Small is the gate AND narrow is the road that leads to life.

WE ALL KNOW THAT THE WAYS OF THE LORD ARE RIGHT

THE Righteous walk in them

BUT

The Rebellious stumble in them!

The world is full of pain and sorrow, this is why it is wise to be righteous and follow the teachings of our LORD JESUS CHRIST. Our LORD knew that there will be a lot of pain in the world. This is why GOD our Father sent him to the world to teach us how to pray to our Father so that our Father can heal our pain. And our LORD JUSUS also experienced the pain of dying on the cross. All He said while He was still waiting for GOD to take His last breath was:—Father, forgive them because they do not know what they are doing. This is why we have to pray for each other, because we are on earth to learn the lessons of life. Let us all be Righteous and not be Rebellious.

LET US LEARN HOW TO PRAY

Prayer must come straight from the Heart, so that our Father can accept our prayer, we must not pray only when we need something or only when we are in trouble. We must pray even when we are happy and thank our Father. The LORDS prayer is one of the healing prayers of all, as it has all the conversation we need to communicate with GOD and it brings us closer to GOD.

THIS is how our LORD taught us to pray

OUR FATHER

WHO art in Heaven

Hallowed be your name

Your Kingdom come

Your Will be done

On Earth as it is in Heaven

Give us this day OUR daily bread

Forgive us our trespasses

As we forgive those who trespass against us

And lead us not into temptation

And deliver us from the evil one

For yours is the Kingdom

The power and the Glory

For ever and ever

Amen

This prayer will help us to learn the ways of our father and help us to be able to forgive each other as the LORD forgave his enemies because He knew that GOD'S purpose has to be fulfilled and these were only the acts of the spirit which needs to evolve to a higher purpose and He also knew that his enemies only hurt the body which was houses the spirit but the spirit itself cannot be hurt because it is protected by GOD. This is why we have to forgive so that our Heavenly Father can also forgive you.

BUT

IF you don't forgive men their sins, our Father will not forgive our sins. We must always remember that our Father can see what is going on in our lives and He is the one who will award accordingly.

Remember that you are not alone, GOD can see, and GOD knows why you are experiencing what you are going through at the moment. Please remember that you are not alone you are reaching the stage of humbleness.

DO YOU FEEL LONELY?

You are not alone GOD is with you,

AND

JESUS CHRIST is bigger than anything we will ever face.

AND; OUR LORD JESUS IS STILL LOOKING AFTER US AND HE CARES A LOT ABOUT US AND HE LOVES US DEARLY. WHAT WE NEED TO DO IS TO FOLLOW HIS TEACHINGS THEN WE WILL LEARN THAT GOD OUR FATHER LOVES US A LOT; AND THIS WHY WE ARE ALL DIFFERENT FROM EACH OTHER. BECAUSE, WE ARE LEARNING DIFFERENT LESSONS AT DIFFERENT TIMES! THIS IS WHY OUR LORD TAUGHT US ABOUT THE FARMER WHO WENT TO SOW HIS SEEDS.

MARK 4:1-9

Jesus began to teach by the lake the crowd that gathered round him, was so large that he got into a bout and sat in it out on the lake, while all the people were along the shore at the water's edge.

He taught them many things by parables and in his teachings said: Listen! A farmer went out sow his seed as he was scattering the seed.

Some fell along the path, and the birds came and ate it up.

Some fell on rocky places, where it did not have much soil. It sprang up quickly, because the soil was shallow. But when the sun came up, the plants were scotched, and they withered because they had no root.

Other seed fell among thorns, which grew up and chocked the plants so that they did not bare grain.

STILL other seed fell on good soil. I t came up. Grew and produced a crop, multiplying thirty six or even a hundred times.

Then JESUS CHRIST said:—He who has ears to hear. Let him hear.

This teaching of our LORD JESUS CHRIST is a very powerful message to all of us. And the disciples were also confused at what our LORD JESUS was talking about and they also asked Him what He meant and that is when our LORD said to them.

"The secret of the Kingdom of GOD is being given to you. But to those on the outside everything is said in parables so that.

They may be ever seeing

BUT

Never perceiving, and ever hearing

BUT

Never understanding;

Otherwise they might turn and be forgiven.

Then JESUS CHRIST realised that the disciples still did not understand what He was trying to tell them.

Then He decided to explain the parable again to them and He said:—The farmer sows the word. Then JESUS explains by saying.

Some people are like seed along the path, where the word is sown. As soon as they hear it' Satan comes and takes away the word that was sown in them.

Others like seed sown on rocky places they hear the word and at once receive it with joy. BUT, since they have no root, they last only a short while, when trouble or persecution comes because of the word, they quickly fall away.

Still others, like seed sown among thorns, hear the word, but the worries of this life the deceitfulness of wealth and desires for other things come in and choke the word, making it unfruitful.

Others, like seed sown on good soil, they hear the word, accept it, and produce a crop—thirty, sixty or even a hundred times what was sown.

PLEASE TAKE NOTE

This parable is very important to all of us to remember what our LORD is teaching us.

The parable of the sower will teach us that we are all not the same, and that we all have our weaknesses and that we must learn to bear with each other. And it teaches us that we must understand each other so that we can be able to teach those who do not understand the meaning of life. And also teaches us to be patient with each other. And mainly to accept each other, and once we can learn to accept each other we will be able to understand the secret of life.

In one of the lessons which I received from the LORD when, the LORD; was teaching me about our seven levels of our spiritual growth. The LORD did tell me that each individual was given a thousand lives for their spiritual growth and these lives were used up through reincarnation, and the lives were given to us so that we can learn all the lessons of life, so that we can reach the highest level which is the seventh level and after we have reached the seventh level we can be able to open the tree of life and the tree of knowledge.

Now this is why our LORD is explaining about the difference between all of us, because the higher the level the more understanding the secret of life and the lower the level is more like having doubts about GOD our Father. And by doubting it only delays our growth.

This book is mainly to remind us about the teaching of the prophets and teachings of our LORD so that we can now prepare ourselves for the coming of the Messiah.

IT is true that we have now reached the end of time. What we need to do is to straighten our ways so that we can gain knowledge about creation.

*   *   *

KNOWLEDGE

He who brings knowledge to others Gains wisdom.

The wise man stores knowledge

We should choose knowledge because Knowledge is the fruit of life.

Knowledge is, understanding

Knowledge is Wisdom

Whoever loves knowledge loves discipline.

Discipline overcomes fear—and overcoming fear brings us close to GOD.

TO OVERCOME FEAR WE MUST EMBRACE GOD

BECAUSE-

GOD IS A HEALER

WE MUST HAVE FAITH IN GOD SO THAT WE CAN REACH THE HIGHER.

REACHING THE HIGHER

WE must remember that we are part of the higher

WE can eventually rise into the higher

AND

Become one there with the higher

THAT is the end and aim of our Revelation

SO that we can help Humanity

THE FOLLOWING TEACHINGS WILL HELP US IN OUR SPIRITUAL JOURNEY. PLEASE READY THEM CAREFULLY AND PRACTISE THEM. We will start learning about how to converse with each other.

TALKING

WHAT EVER WE SAY

WE

MUST THINK BEFORE WE SAY IT!

* * *

THINKING

WE MUST LEARN TO THINK QUICKLY AND ACT PROMTLY

AND

YET WITH CONSIDERATION

*   *   *

EVIL DEEDS

Evil deeds will always bring pain to all of us

Victim and Perpetrator!

Let us read the words of the teacher who teaches us about sin and sorrow. This is what he says to us.

SIN AND SORROW

However Terrible Sin and Sorrow on Earth

ALL

Lessons are somehow working together

FOR

The good of all

AND

Humanity is being slowly guided towards Its Final Goal.

This why we have to share the gift of wisdom with each other:—So that we can be able to seek the face of GOD so that He can heal our wounds.

Because

WISDOM IS SHARED NOT SOLD

2 CHRONICLES 7:14-16

If my people, who are called by my name, will humble themselves and pray and seek my face and from their wicked ways, then will I hear from Heaven and will forgive their sin and will heal their land.

Now my eyes will be open and my ears attentive to the prayers offered in this place. I have chosen and consecrated this temple so that my name may be there for ever. My eyes and my heart will always be there.

This is the promise to us from GOD our Father. Now let us build the temple of the LORD in us, so that we can enjoy the love of GOD and share the love of GOD with each other.

THE ACT OF LOVE

We see GOD in every act of love

AND

Compassion that Graces our Lives

WE can join GOD in offering compassion and tears to all those who suffer today. And we must give to the needy all the time because in our past lives we were also given what we needed at the time we needed it, by those who felt compassion for us. Now! It is our time to be compassionate.

THE COMPASSION IN GIVING

We must give completely with love

AND

THE World will give completely to us!

* * *

THE WAY TO CHRIST

Is to draw close to those the world avoids!

*   *   *

PLEASE TAKE NOTE

Our LORD has taught us many times that we must love each other. Now it is the time that we should care for each other, because caring for each other is our duty and it is GOD'S purpose we will be fulfilling.

IMPERFECTION

Because we are all imperfect beings and we still have to be fully Developed Spiritually that means we still guidance from the LORD and GOD OUR FATHER.

ALL we need to do is, to ask our comforter to lead us and teach us. Then, our comforter will bring the right people closer to us, so that they can teach us whatever we are ready to learn. Our LORD IS OUR COMFORTER.

JESUS CHRIST CAN CALM THE STORMS IN OUR LIVES

EVEN

WHEN HEALING DOES NOT COME

AND

FINDING COMFORT IN OUR LORD JESUS CHRIST

IT IS

ALLOWING GOD'S WILL IN OUR LIVES

*   *   *

When we open up to GOD he will direct us to places where we will be able to learn our life lessons and to fulfil His purpose. This is why now and again we find ourselves living in different countries which we never thought of in our lives and never even heard of until we find ourselves placed in these strange places and completely accepting the situation even though we are not happy being called names or aliens because we are being directed by the spirit of GOD:—So that we can learn our lessons and fulfil the purpose of GOD. This is why we have to be righteous all the time. GOD does not place us in these places so that we can commit evil deeds. He sends us so that we can be able to share our wisdom with each other. It is all about serving humanity with love not about destroying humanity.

IT IS ALWAYS GOD'S WILL

We must remember

THAT

GOD chooses places

AT

Which His grace will be especially active

AND

GOD makes us to be attached to such places

AND

To visit them frequently

AND

TO pray there for the help we need in our weaknesses.

AND

Prayer; will increase our faith in GOD.

$$* \quad * \quad *$$

HEBREWS 11: 1

Faith is being sure of what we hope and certain of what we do not see.

PLEASE TAKE NOTE

IT does not mean that if we can't see GOD we can't have faith in Him. Having faith in GOD our Father will help us to heal, and healing will teach us to forgive others.

LET US LEARN THE AWARDS OF FORGIVENESS

LUKE 17; 3-4

If your brother sins rebuke him

AND

If he repents forgive him

If he Sins against you seven times in a day

AND

Seven times comes to you and says I repent

FORGIVE HIM

BY forgiving each other will bring us closer to perfection and help us find the path which leads us back home to our father.

Because;—Our spirit is longing for perfection.

THE BEST WAY TO REACH PERFECTION IS TO AIM FOR PERFECTION. THIS WHAT THE BIBLE TEACHES US ALL THE TIME.

THE COMFORT OF PERFECTIION

2 CORINTHAINS

Aim for perfection Listen to my appeal

BE of one in mind and live in peace with each other

AND

The love of GOD will be with you

THE love of GOD will bring us closer to each other and we will become one with each other again.

Let us now learn about boasting because boasting is the inventor of jealousy.

BOASTING THE INVENTOR OF JEALOUSY

1 CORINTHIANS 5; 6-7

Your boasting is not good:—Don't you know that a little yeast works through the Whole batch of dough!

Get rid of the old yeast: That you may be the batch without yeast.

* * *

LET US NOW GET RID OF JEALOUSY
JEALOUSY THE SUSPENSION
OF
OUR SPIRITUAL GROWTH

1CORINTHIANS 3:1

I could not address you as spiritual but as worldly mere infants in CHRIST.

I gave you milk not solids, for you were not yet ready for it. Indeed, you are still worldly,

For, since there is jealousy and quarrelling among you, are You not worldly?

Are you not acting like mere man?

For when one says I follow Paul and another says, I follow Apollos. Are you not mere man?

PLEASE TAKE NOTE

Apostle Paul is teaching us about jealousy, it is true that jealousy is a killer it is the killer of the spirit, because when we are unhappy with ourselves this is when we start building up jealousy in us, and at the end that jealousy turns to anger, then anger turns to murder. This is why we need to be religious. RELIGION IS WHAT OUR SPIRIT IS SEEKING FOR BECAUSE IT IS FOOD FOR THE SOUL.

HOW CAN OUR SPIRIT REACH THE HIGHER DIMENTION

WHEN

IT IS NOT FED WELL?

HOW CAN OUR BODIES SURVIVE LIFE

WHEN THE BODY LACKS NUTRITION AND NOT FED WELL!

As it is with the body it is the same with the spirit both needs to be fed well to be able to survive.

Religion is the nutrition for the spirit.

RELIGIONS

The message from the Apostle Paul which we have just read;—it brings to mind about, the teaching of different Religions. Here the apostle Paul is trying to teach us that we should be spiritual. Which means;—we must believe in GOD, and we must learn from all the Prophets of different Religions as they all have different gifts of teaching from the one and only GOD who is one creator the universe.

It does not mean our particular religion is better than another, because when we see it like that. We will forget about the purpose of life, which is our spiritual journey.

Our spiritual journey is meant to take us back to GOD our father in Heaven, which is what our spirit is longing for, and the spirit knows that it does not belong to earth and the spirit does not want to belong to earth at all.

Our spirit is only here on earth to learn the lessons of life not to belong where it does not belong. So by being jealousy and having pride and thinking we are better than each other it is only a waste of life.

We all have seen that everything evil thing we do to each, only brings a lot of pain from one generation to the next and it gets worse by a minute. So now is the time for each individual to find their spiritual journey and learn the lessons of life with love. Then the bond of evil will leave us and we will become Spiritual all jealousy and hatred will not take part in our lives. Only faith will lead us to the narrow road that leads to LIFE.

*   *   *

FAITH

LUKE 17: 6

IF you have faith as small as a mustard seed—You can say—To this mulberry tree, be rooted and planted AND—It will obey you.

FAITH

HEBREWS 11:30

By faith the walls of Jericho fell—-After—The people had matched around them For seven days.

FAITH

Your faith must not rest on men's wisdom

BUT

On GOD'S power because—GOD is love

* * *

GOD

GOD IS LOVE BEYOND LOVE

LOVE MUST BE SINCERE

LOVE:—REJOICE WITH THOSE WHO REJOCE

MOURN:—MOURN WITH THOSE WHO MOURN

LIVE IN HARMONY WITH ONE ANOTHER

LOVE MUST BE SINCERE AND CLING TO WHAT IS GOOD

PLEASE NOTE

WIthout faith in GOD we are like lost sheep. The only way to find our way back is in prayer. The LORD said to u:—NEVER WILL I LEAVE YOU AND NEVER WILL I FORSAKE YOU.

HEBREWS 11:8

BY faith Abraham when called to go to a place he would later receive as his inheritance, obeyed and went even though he did not know where he was going.

FAITH IN WORDS

THERE is guidance for all of us—BY Listening we shall hear the right words and these words will shine a light of GOD which is within us.

THE LIGHT OF GOD

The LORD is our light—and our salvation—the strength of our light will help us to fear nothing because GOD is our shield and He will protect us.

PART TWO=[3]

LEARNING THE LAWS OF DEVOTION

GENISIS 15: 1

Do not be Afraid Abraham

I am your shield

YOUR

EVERY GREAT REWARD

PLEASE TAKE NOTE

These words of comfort are not meant only for Abraham they are meant for all of us, as we all know that we are all the descendants of Abraham.

Abraham is our Earth father

And

GOD is our spiritual Father.

Whatever messages which our Earth Father Abraham received in his past life it is still the laws which we need to acknowledge in our lives and our future lives and keep to these laws of GOD which were passed through Abraham our Father. So that we can be able to travel a smooth journey:—Because GOD is the spirit in us.

GOD IS SPIRIT

JOHN 4: 2

GOD IS SPIRIT AND HIS WORSHIPPERS

MUST

WORSHIP IN SPIRIT AND TRUTH!

*   *   *

JOHN 4:23

Yet the time is coming—AND—Has now come

When

The worshippers will worship—The Father in spirit and truth

FOR

THEY ARE THE KIND THE FATHER SEEKS

We must trust in GOD and not lose hope.

WORDS OF COURAGE

HEBREWS 12: 5-6

My son do not make light of the LORD'S discipline.

AND

Do not lose Heart when He rebukes you!

BECAUSE

The LORD disciplines those He loves.

AND

He punishes everyone He accepts as Sons.

* * *

We are the sons of GOD and because we are GOD'S children He has the right to lead us to the right path. Just; like you lead your child to be righteous by teaching him words of wisdom.

MATHEW 18:12-13

IF a man owns a hundred sheep and one of them wonders away. Will he not leave the ninety nine on the hill and go to look for the one that wondered off:—AND if he finds it; I tell you the truth, he is happier about that one sheep, than about the ninety nine that did not wonder.

All we need to do is to pray for each other so that they can find the way back home.

HOW TO BECOME SONS OF GOD

THE TEN STEPS TO RIGHTEOUSNESS

We must keep on praying.

WE must have respect for each other.

WE must learn to forgive.

WE must always tell the truth.

WE must not keep bad secrets.

WE must not be misled by others.

WE must discard evil doing.

WE must think before we act.

WE must live a clean life.

WE must forgive each other!

*   *   *

EZEKIAL 18: 4

FOR EVERY LIVING SOUL

BELONGS TO GOD

Because we all belong to GOD that makes us twin brothers and by becoming brothers in love that will help us understand GOD our Father. Then:—when we understand the ways of our Father that brings humanity to the world because humanity is a twin sister of peace.

HUMANITY IS A TWIN SISTER OF PEACE

HUMANITY

HEBREWS 13:1-3

KEEP on loving each other!

REMEMBER those in prison as if—You were their fellow prisoner.

And

Those who are ill—As if you are ill yourself!

And

Those who are ill—treated—as if—you yourself were suffering!

It is true that we must care for each other and feel each other's pain than criticising each other and this means we have to learn to share our pain with each other.

SHARING OUR PAIN

Sharing our grief and fears will surely encourage others to the do the same and this will lighten our life purpose. And we will then become merciful to those who are still searching for the right path.

BE MERCIFUL

JUDE 1: 22-23

Be merciful to those who doubt.

Snatch others from the fire and save them.

To others show mercy, mixed with fear—Hating even the clothing stained by corrupted flesh.

When we start to hate evil we will reduce temptation which corrupts confuses our minds.

TEMPTATION

TEMPTATION LEADS TO DESIRE

AND

DESIRE—LEADS TO SIN

AND

SIN—GIVES BIRTH TO DEATH ONCE FULL GROWN!

LET US LEARN ABOUT FAVOURITISM

JAMES 2:1-4

As believers in our glorious LORD JESUS CHRIST, don't show favouritism. Suppose a man comes into your meeting wearing a gold ring and fine clothes. And a poor man in shabby clothes also comes in.

IF you show special attention to the man wearing fine clothes and say, here is a good seat for you. But say to the poor man, you stand there . . . or sit on the floor by my feet.

Have you not discriminated among yourselves and become judges with evil thoughts.

JAMES 2:5-7

Listen, my dear brothers; has, not GOD chosen those who are poor in the eyes of the world to be rich in faith and inherit the Kingdom he promised those who love him.

But you have insulted the poor. Is it not the rich who are exploiting you?

Are they not the ones who are dragging you into court?

Are they not the ones who are slandering the noble name of whom you belong?

IF you really keep the royal law found in scripture, Love your neighbours as yourself. You are doing right.

But

If you show favouritism, you sin and are convicted by the law as law breakers.

For whoever keeps the whole law and yet stumbles at just one point, is guilty of breaking all of it.

For he who said, Do, not commit adultery. Also said:—Do not murder

If you do not commit adultery but do commit murder, you have become a law breaker.

Speak and act as those who are going to be judged by the law that gives freedom, because judgement without mercy will be shown to anyone who has not been merciful.

<u>MECRY TRIUMPHS OVER JUDGEMENT</u>

<u>PLEASE TAKE NOTE</u>

Now we have learned about favouritism, it is true what we have learned. Because this is what is happening in the world, and it is not worth it, especially if it is going to limit our spiritual growth and keep us away from reaching our promised land. So favouritism is just a waste of time and a waste of life.

Favouritism comes in many different forms

[A] Discrimination amongst Cultures

[B] Discrimination amongst Countries

[C] Discrimination against Colour

[D] Discrimination in the families

[E] Discrimination amongst our own Children

[F] Judging others

[G] Discriminating against other Religions

There are so many ways which we continuously use to discriminate against each other and that is favouritism. So it is time we stop it, so that we can be able to find the way back home.

<u>DO YOU REMEMBER THE MAGIC WORD:—DO NOT TAKE THE WORLD FOR YOUR HOME YOU ARE ONLY ON EARTH TO LEARN THE LESSONS OF LIFE. YOUR HOME IS IN HEAVEN AND TO REACH HEAVEN WE MUST BE LIKE CHILDREN.</u>

LET US BECOME LIKE LITTLE CHILDREN

MATTHEW 18:1-6

At the time the disciples came to JESUS and asked:—Who is the greatest in the Kingdom of Heaven? JESUS called a little child and had him stand among them. And He said; I tell you the truth, unless you change and become like little children, you will never enter the Kingdom of Heaven.

Therefore who ever humbles himself like this little child is the greatest in the Kingdom of Heaven.

And whoever welcomes a little child like this in my name welcomes me.

BUT!

IF anyone causes one of these little ones, who believe in me to sin, it will be better for him to have a large millstone hung around his neck and to be drowned in the depths of the sea.

We have now learned about how we can enter the Kingdom of heaven. That really means that we should be like little children, because, the little children are pure in heart and they are able to hear the voice of GOD when He talks to them.

NOW let us learn how to listen to the voice of GOD.

JOB 33:-12-18

For GOD is greater than man. Why do you complain to Him, that He answers none of man's words?

For GOD does speak—now one way, now another!

Though; man may not perceive it.

In a dream . . . . In a vision of the night

When deep sleep falls on man

As they slumber in their beds—He may speak in their ears

AND

Terrify them with warnings—To turn man from wrongdoing.

And

Keep him from pride—To preserve his soul from the pit.

And

His life from perishing by the sword!

Yes! We must listen to the voice of GOD because now and again GOD talks to us. If we can be able to hear the voice of GOD will be able to share our love with each other.

LET US LEARN ABOUT LOVE

ROMANS12:9-13

Love must be sincere.

Hate what is Evil.

Cling to what is good.

Be devoted to one another in brotherly love.

Honour one another above yourselves.

Never be lacking in zeal—but—Keep your spiritual fervour, serving the LORD.

HOPE—PATIENCE AND FAITH

BE JOYFUL IN HOPE

PATIENCE IN AFFLICTION

FAITH IN PRAYER

DO NOT REPAY EVIL FOR EVIL!

HOW TO OVERCOME EVIL

ROMANS 12:17-20

Do not repay anyone evil for evil.

Be careful to do what is right in the eyes of everybody.

IF it is possible, as far as it depends on you—Live at peace with everyone.

Do not take revenge—BUT—Leave room for GOD'S wrath for it is written:—It is mine to avenge. I will repay, says the LORD.

IF your enemy is hungry; . . . . Feed him

IF he is thirsty; . . . Give him something to drink

IN doing so, you will heap burning coals in his head.

Do not be overcome by Evil!

But

Overcome Evil.

OVERCOMING EVIL LEADS TO THE RIVER OF LIFE.

LET US NOW LEARN ABOUT SIN

The soul that sin—Is the one who will die.

The son—Will not share the guilt of the father.

No will—The father; share the guilt of the son.

YES! It is true! At the end of time when, the LORD comes to award us; He will judge each individual at the time chosen by the LORD. Each individual will be accountable for his deeds.

ROMANS 14:11-12

IT is written:—As surely as I live, says the LORD

Every knee will bow down to me.

Every tongue will confess to GOD

PLEASE NOTE

Each of us will give account of himself to GOD. We must start to practice good deeds so that we can be ready for the coming of the LORD. And once we have learned the laws of righteousness we will live a happy life.

LET US LEARN HOW TO STAY HAPPINESS

These three words which are:—[1] Faith—[2] Hope and[3] Courage will lead us to everlasting happiness.

WHEN we are happy we will be able to be like the seed which fell on good soil, which is the man who hears the word and understands it. He produces a crop, yielding a hundred, sixty or thirty times what was sown. Matthew 13:23.

LET US NOW LEARN
HOW TO BECOME THE SEED
WHICH
FELL ON GOOD SOIL

*   *   *

This next reading will teach us how to communicate with GOD.

EXODUS 33:13

Moses said to the LORD; LORD if you are pleased with me. Teach me your ways so I may know you and continue to find favour with you.

EXODUS 33: 17

The LORD said to Moses, I will do the very thing you have asked, because, I am pleased with you and I know you by name.

Then Moses said, now, show me your glory."

And

The LORD said, I will cause all my goodness to pass in front of you, and I will proclaim my name, the LORD in your presence.

I will have mercy on whom, I will have mercy.

I will have compassion on whom, I will have compassion.

BUT

The LORD said; you cannot see my face. For no—one may see me and live.

Then the LORD said; there is a place near me where you may stand on the rock. When my glory passes by, I will out you in a cleft in a rock and cover you with my hand until I have passed by. Then I will remove my hand and you will see my back; but my face must not be seen.

PLEASE NOTE

We have now read the wonderful conversation between Moses and GOD. It is true that if we ask GOD to lead us to the right path. GOD our Father is always willing to do so and if we ask GOD our Father to forgive us, GOD our Father is always ready to forgive us.

Let us be like Moses who had Faith in GOD

AND

Let us be like Moses who had courage to ask GOD for help.

AND

Let us be the seed which fell on good soil

We must all remember that GOD still works through all of us, now and again GOD will choose amongst us his messengers to update what needs to be updated.

AND

TO teach us what needs to be taught at the time GOD chooses.

AND

TO confirm what needs to be confirmed in the world.

So we must not argue with the prophets of today thinking that they come from the devil. The devil only teaches Evil, the prophets and messengers of GOD will only confirm what is written in the BIBLE and what GOD our Father taught them to confirm to us and explain some of the parables which we did not understand when JESUS CHRIST was teaching.

Let us all learn the teachings of the prophets and keep to their teachings. We all know what is wrong and what is right, so let's choose the right things in life.

LET US NOW LEARN

HOW

TO LIVE A PEACEFUL LIFE.

1 THESSALONIANS 4:11-12

Make it your ambition to lead quiet life, to mind your own business, and to work with your hands, just as we told you.

So that your, daily life may win the respect of outsiders.

AND

So, that, you will not be depended on anybody.

PLEASE TAKE NOTE

Apostle Paul is teaching us, how to live a quiet life and minding our own business, he is right because most of the time we spend our time judging people around us, and just making our lives impossible to bare and spend our nights in fear of what we assumed to be. Yet time is going by, when we could be preparing ourselves for the coming of the LORD or the end of our day on earth.

We all know that we can never predict the time when each of us will live this world. We have watched our beloved ones and friends die in front of our eyes and we still fail to understand the ways of our LORD. Let each individual find their purpose before their time comes to live this world, because we cannot take our burdens with us, but; we can take the light of GOD with us. And the light of GOD will direct us back to our Father.

I myself know that GOD our Father is there waiting for us, because He chose me to be one of his messengers and I am very pleased to fulfil my Fathers purpose. You must also be ready for your calling from GOD our Father because only GOD knows the time when He will call on you.

MAY THE LOVE OF GOD

BE

WITH ALL GOD'S CHILDREN

We have learned that GOD has a plan for all of us. So let us live in peace with each other.

BECAUSE

GOD is at peace with all of us.

GOD ALWAYS TELLS ME HOW MUCH HE LOVES US

AND

GOD WANTS US ALL TO KNOW HOW COMPASSIONATE HE IS TO ALL OF US!

EPHESIANS 1:11-14

In Him we were also chosen having been predestined according to the plan of him who works out everything in conformity with the purpose of His will.

In order that, we who were the first to hope in CHRIST, might be for the praise of His Glory.

And you also were included in CHRIST when you heard the word of truth, the gospel of your salvation.

Having believed you were marked in Him with a seal, the promised Holy Spirit, who is a deposit guaranteeing our inheritance until the redemption of those who are GOD'S possession—to the praise of His Glory!

PLEASE TAKE NOTE

The words of the Apostle Paul are good teachings they will lead us to perfection, as we have now understood that we are marked with the Holy Spirit. These words should give us courage to keep on fulfilling GOD'S purpose, which is to serve Humanity with love, and this will guarantee our safe journey to Heaven.

We have now learned and confirmed what GOD our Father wants us to live. And we all know that, if we live a good life and avoid unnecessary temptations we are sure to enter the Kingdom of Heaven.

LET US LEARN ABOUT TRIALS TEMPTATIONS

JAMES 1:1-8

To the twelve tribes scattered among the nations.

TRIALS AND TEMPTATIONS

Consider it pure joy my brother's whenever you face trails of many kinds. Because you know that your testing of your faith develops perseverance. Perseverance must finish its work so that you may be mature and complete, not lacking anything.

IF any of you lacks wisdom, he should ask GOD, who gives generously to all without finding fault, and it will be given to him.

BUT

When he asks he must believe and not doubt.

BECAUSE

He who doubts is like a wave of the sea, blown and tossed by the wind.

That man should not think he will receive anything from the LORD. He is a double-minded man, unstable in all he does.

PLEASE TAKE NOTE

Thanks to James the servant of GOD who knows what he is talking about; he does not speak about the past only. He also speaks about the future which is the now and the next. Every word he teaches; it is the confirmation of what will always take place through generation and generations until the end of time.

JAMES knows that every generation will have to learn the lessons of life until we all reach perfection and he also knows that some people will doubt the words of GOD and they will become impatient and turn away from the LORD, but he spends his time teaching us to have faith in GOD and not to give up on GOD.

As we all know that at this time of the millennium, most of the people are going through so much pain and most of the people have lost most of what they have worked hard for. James;—teaches us that, now and again some people will go through a test and when some people experience trials in their lives, that means it is the time for them to be tested and the test is meant to increase their faith in GOD. This is what is going on in every part of the world at this moment, the rich losing their hard work and becoming desolate.

BUT

Then James tells us that we must rejoice whenever we face trials of many kinds, because our faith is being tested.

YES; I am one of those who were tested in the year two thousand and six [2006]. That is the time when I did not realised that it was GOD who was testing my faith. I spent a few years it tears crying for everything which was taken from me, which was everything which I worked hard for years and years. I was left with nothing at all, but God never failed to protect me and talking to me explaining what was going on in the world. And telling me what He wants me to do for Him.

I still feel a slight pain now and again when I think about my hard work which I worked hard for years and years hoping to reach my retirement without being a burden to my children. But faith in GOD kept me alive and now I am busy working for the LORD as He asked me to work for Him and teach about what we should do to prepare ourselves for the end of time.

Now I have nothing, even to buy a cool drink, but my daughters are looking after me. Now and again I feel that it is unfair for GOD to do such a terrible test to all good people, but; I realised that if I did not go through such a test I wouldn't know that GOD my Father is still with us and I wouldn't know that; that man on the street who is homeless is a child of GOD who was put on the street to be a mirror to us, and he also needs a home like all of us do. But his journey is a different journey to us. He is put there so that we can learn from him. Just like Judas who was made to betray our LORD so that the scripture can be fulfilled.

Now that I am in the same position with the poor homeless man I know how it feels. I have learned how it is to be rich and how it is to be poor. If I did not lose everything which was worth millions and millions and ended up with no money no Home no Job because I was put in a bad credit record which I did not deserve because All what I had was stolen from me.

BUT; thanks to GOD who was always close to me, and our LORD JESUS CHRIST who was always with me and the Angels who were protecting me, and thanks to the poor people whom I met on the streets who shared their life stories with me and thanks to the people who were rich like me and lost everything they earned just like me and shared their pain with me.

All these people increased my faith in GOD and helped me to humble myself, and when I became humble the LORD came to talk to me.

Please believe me all those who are experiencing pain. It will all go to pass because in life when you lose something you gain something.

I lost the Earthly things

But

I have gained Heavenly.

The Heavenly things are gifts which come from the Father and I have gained love for all and I am at peace with GOD'S creation. I am now one with creation I am now a child of GOD and I will never let go the cross I am holding on, because I have never been so happy in my life.

The riches brought me happiness, pain, stress, anger, frustration, enemy's and all sorts of hatred and confusions.

Now I am free, I am now one with all GOD creation and everything I see is a mirror of me and it is wonderful.

Because everything is a mirror of me I cannot hate myself or criticize myself, and it is great.

All I can do—is to love what I see in the mirror.

IF I don't like what I see in the mirror"

I pray to GOD my Father to embrace it and give it love.

Thanks to the James the servant of GOD

AND

OUR LORD JESUS

May the blessings of GOD our Father stay in you forever

PRAISE BE TO GOD OUR FATHER

TO HEAR THE VOICE OF GOD WE MUST BE HUMBLE. THE BOOK OF JAMES IN THE BIBLE TEACHES US TO HUMBLE OURSELVES.

WE MUST HUMBLE OUR SELVES

JAMES 1: 9-12

The brother in humble circumstances ought to take pride in his high position.

BUT

The one who is rich should take part in his low position, because he will pass away like a wild flower. For the sun rises with scorching heat and withers the plant. Its blossom falls and its beauty is destroyed.

IN the same way, the rich man will fade away even while he goes about his business.

Blessed is the man who perseveres under trail. Because when he has stood the test, he will receive the crown of life that GOD has promised to those who love Him.

PLEASE NOTE

We have learned that our trials we are going through no matter how painful they are. It is only to strengthen our faith. And we must persevere, because if we do we will receive our award. We have received good news we must not fear, because GOD is always with us.

HEBREWS 13: 2

Keep on loving each other as brothers. Do not forget to entertain strangers, for by so doing.

Some people have entertained Angels without knowing it.

Remember those in prison as if you were their fellow-prisoners and those who are ill-treated as if you yourself were suffering.

MATTHEW 10:28

Do not be afraid of those who kill the body

But

Cannot kill the soul!

Rather

Be afraid of the one who can destroy both Soul and Body in Hell.

PLEASE NOTE

These words you are about to read are the words written by our Priest in ST Georges church in Cape-Town South Africa. Father Rowan Smith is a servant of GOD and He knows the ways of our Father, he is always ready to answer every question we asked him with a big smile on his face and with words which are full of love. I have never seen him angry since I have known him and I have met a lot of people who tell wonderful testimony's about Father Rowan.

I have also become one of the people who have a lot of wonderful words to say about this great servant of GOD. The words we are about to read were written by Father Rowan Smith and they light up the world with all sort of beautiful things. Which are visible and invisible to the eye:—

The visible are the things of the Body

And

The invisible are the things of the Spirit.

He sees the splendour of GODS creation as an awesome world.

THIS AWESOME WORLD

We live In an awesome world

Make it An awesome day

And

Give—Love and peace to all!

Live simply:—Love dearly:—Care deeply

And

LEAVE THE REST TO GOD!

These are wonderful words coming from our Vicar:—The Revered ROWAN SMITH

FROM ST GEORGES CATHEDRAL CAPE TOWN

THANK, YOU FATHER ROWAN SMITH.

PLEASE NOTE

You might wonder when I said Father Rowan's words will light up the world with all sorts of things, which are visible and invisible.

[1] <u>The visible things</u> as I have explained are the things we see in the world whether good or bad. And we have to be embraced both. This is what it says in this poem:—We live in an awesome world and make it an awesome day and give Love to all. That's what I call food for the Spirit.

[2] The invisible things as I have explained are the things of the Spirit, which the Spirit is longing for. This is what it says in the poem:—Live simply—Love dearly—Care deeply and live all to GOD.

WONDERFUL WORDS THANKS AGAIN FATHER ROWAN.

When we follow these wonderful words of Father Rowan Smith, we will enjoy both the journey of the spirit and the lessons of life. And the LORD will open our eyes so we can be able to see beyond the mystery of Life.

JOHN 9:1-26

As JESUS CHRIST went along, he saw a man blind from birth. His disciples asked him, "Rabbi, who sinned this man or his parent, that he was born blind?

Neither this man nor his parent sinned; said JESUS "but, this happened so that the work of GOD might be displayed in life. As long as it is day we must do the work of Him who sent me. Night is coming, when no one can work. While I am in the world I am the light of the world.

Having said this He spat on the ground, made some mud with the saliva, and put it on the man's eyes. Go He told him wash in the pool Siloam. So the man went and washed and came home seeing.

PLEASE TAKE NOTE

The reading of the book of[John9: 1-26] clearly opens our eyes, it teaches us that we are on earth to learn the lessons of life and that only our LORD can open our eyes only when we have learned to believe in him.

To receive the light of GOD which will reveal GOD our Father to us; is to trust in the LORD JESUS CHRIST.

PART FOUR [4]

WHICH;—IS CALLED THE DELAYED BOOK OF LAWS IS ABOUT LEARNING HOW TO OVERCOME EVIL DEEDS

Part four brings us back to remembering the laws of Moses which GOD instructed us from the beginning of time these laws taught us to be able to differentiate between good and evil. The laws of Moses are the laws which our LORD JESUS CHRIST has asked me to right down on this book so that we can now start to practice and live our lives according to these teachings because we have now learned the lessons of life through reincarnation and we are able to distinguish between good and bad.

This will prepare us for the end of time as our sins have now been cleansed after <u>a thousand lives </u>of our life lessons and <u>a thousand years</u> of learning our life lessons and learning how to fulfil our life purpose. Now it is the time to test our faith and this is why the devil is released to the world mainly to test us at the end of our journey. Our sins have been cleansed and we are now about to receive our awards.

PLEASE TAKE NOTE

This is not a joke it is real. Some may ignore these messages but it is up to them. My advice is:—just start living a good life and discard evil deeds because we are all going to experience a lot of pain in the world. The disasters we see happening now in the world cannot be compared with the future. The future is going to be worse than what we are experiencing at this time and the pain is going to be intense. This is what the LORD has told me to tell the world.

It does not matter who you are or what position you hold in this world. Each individual is going through a spiritual test. And no one can stop what is going to take place. We are now on our second stage of the End of the world.

THE FOUR STAGES
OF
THE END OF TIME

The first [stage1] stage; was the testing of our faith when the devil got released in the year two thousand and five [2005] to come and test us. The devil was locked up after a few years in the year [2009] but then his evil deeds are still being practised in the world to test those who are still to be tested. And this first stage lasted for six years [6] which was from the year two thousand and five [2005] to two thousand and eleven [2011]. During the testing GOD was anointing some of the good people who have served him well and mind you:—The devil was also putting a mark on his chosen ones marking them with a number six on their fore-head. And that gave the devil his first six [6].

The second stage [stage2] of the end of the world is the cleansing of sins which will take place from the year twenty twelve[2012] and takes another six years till the year two thousand and seventeen[2017] and while GOD is busy cleansing the world of sin and anointing more of His people during these six years [6] the devil was also busy marking his own people on their for-head with a number six[6] and that gives the devil his second number six[6].

The third stage [stage3] of the end of the world is the transformation which will take place from the year two thousand and seventeen until the year two thousand and twenty three[2023]which gives us six years[6] of transformation time for those who are still in the world. While GOD is busy transforming His good people who have served Him well during the six years, the devil will also mark his people with a mark on their fore-head which will be the third six[6] on their fore-head. Which makes the devils number which is the three sixes [666].

The fourth stage [stage4] of the end of the world is the time when the LORD sends the prophet who will come and help those who are still in the world struggling to change their ways. The messenger of the LORD who is the spirit of Josiah will only help these people only for two years and he will be very harsh with these people because they would have experienced the wrath of GOD by then and this will be their last chance to change their ways; otherwise the devil will be waiting to take them with him as the devil is always happy to have a good crowd with him. This stage will only last for two years [2]. Which gives us until the year two thousand and twenty five [2025] and then this is what is called the END OF THE WORLD when the LORD comes to collect all the last good people left on earth.

This is it! It all sounds crazy but, I don't think so because all these messages came from the LORD and there has been a lot of work going through from the last six years [6]. GOD CREATED THE WORLD IN SIX DAYS AND RESTED ON THE SEVENTH DAY. And the book took six years and now the world will read it on the seventh year. NOW: I UNDERSTAND WHY THE LORD CALLS THIS MESSAGE THE DELAYED BOOK OF LAWS.

PART FIVE [5]

LEARNING HOW TO OVERCOME EVIL
FROM
THE DELAYED BOOK OF LAWS

<u>PLEASE DO NOT WASTE TIME—BE REAL AND DO THE RIGHT THIN!</u>

The book of laws is to remind us, of how to live a fulfilling life without pain and guilt or worry. It teaches us that the ways of living according to the teachings of religion are true and if we live according to these teachings we will be able to see the Kingdom of GOD.

It was after I finished writing the book of messages which I received from the LORD. The title of the book is called:—LET'S CELEBRATE THE END AND DANCE TO THE MUSIC OF TIME.

After writing the book, the LORD told me that I should write the book of laws but, the title of the book should be called <u>THE DELAYED BOOK OF LAWS</u>. Please don't ask me why the book is called the delayed book of laws. All I can say to you is; the LORD has an amazing sense of humour.

When the LORD was teaching me how to write the first book of messages He always joked with me and we both shared a good laugh. It was me and my spiritual teacher and the cherub Jude and the LORD working together. We had a wonderful time working together and, it was great.

The LORD is full of love. He taught me how to love and appreciate all of GOD'S Creation. I hope that when you finish reading the delayed book of laws. You will learn that from the beginning of creation human beings made mistakes and when the guilt destroys them, they turn to blame GOD. But GOD wrote the laws for us and also sent the prophets to us, so that they can give us messages from GOD, but we completely ignore these messages from GOD and we go according to what pleases us.

That is when the trouble starts, because we are not following the teachings of the LORD. This is why the LORD asked me to re-write the teachings of the prophets, so that we can prepare ourselves for the end of time, because now the LORD is getting ready to open the doors of Heaven for us and He would like all of us to be able to go back to our Home in Heaven and be with our Father.

Please try and find the book which I have written which will explain to you about our spiritual journey and you will learn that GOD our FATHER is really a loving GOD, and you will also learn that we all come from the same GOD and we were only on earth to learn the lessons of life and to fulfil GOD'S purpose with love.

Then you will learn that we are all students who were given different teacher's to teach us different lessons for the purpose of our spiritual growth.

You will also learn that we were also given a thousand lives for each individual soul to learn the lessons of life. And the book clearly explains that each one of us is here on earth to learn all the lessons of life, and this is why GOD gave us a thousand lives to learn all the lessons of life. The book will also teach you about reincarnation and that it is true that when we die we do discard our old bodies and when we come back for our next lesson, GOD gives us a new body which is suitable for our next lesson.

Now you will learn that we are all old souls which have been in and out of earth and now it is the time for JUDGEMENT. This book of laws which, the LORD asked me to write it is to remind us of the teachings of the LORD and the teachings of all religions and confirming the end of time.

Please read the teachings of our LORD and live your life according to the teachings of the laws of GOD. We all learned that there is time for everything. Now it is time to discard all evildoing, and this book will remind us about what are evil things so that we can change evil to good.

The delayed book of laws is mainly to prepare us for the end of time.

LET US LEARN FROM DANIEL THE MESSANGER OF GOD.

Daniel 12:1-13

At that time Michael, the great prince who protects your people will arise. There will be a time of distress such as has not happened from the beginning of nations until then.

But at that time your people—everyone whose name is written in the book—will be delivered.

Multitude—who sleep in the dust of the earth will awake; some to everlasting life, others to shame and everlasting contempt.

Those who are wise will shine like the brightness of the Heavens,

AND

Those who lead many to righteousness like the stars for ever and ever.

Then GOD said to Daniel; but you Daniel, close up and seal the words of the scroll until the time of the end. Many will go here and there to increase knowledge.

Then I Daniel looked and there before me stood two others, one on this bank of the river and one on the opposite bank. One of them said to the man clothed in linen, who was about the waters of the river.

How long will it be before these astonishing things are fulfilled?

The man clothed in linen, who was above the waters of the river, lifted his right hand and his left hand towards Heaven, and I heard him swear by him who lives forever saying, it will be for a time, times and a half time.

When the power of the Holy people has been finally broken, all these things will be completed.

Daniel says; I heard but did not understand. So I asked; My LORD what will the outcome of this be?

The LORD replied; Go your way Daniel because the words are closed up and sealed until the time of the end.

Many will be purified, made spotless and refined.

But

The wicked will continue to be wicked. None of the wicked will understand, but those who are wise will understand.

From the time that the daily sacrifice is abolished and the abomination that causes desolation is set up, there will be 1,290 days, and reaches the end of the 1,335 days.

As for you, go your way till the end. You will rest, and then at the end of the days you will rise to receive your allotted inheritance.

PLEASE TAKE NOTE

Well—we can hear what Daniel has told us. Daniels messages are true, as we can all see what is taking place in the world. And the LORD did say to Daniel that he must close up and seal the words of the scroll until the time of the end. And the LORD also said many will go here and there to increase the knowledge. Yes" it is true because one of the messages which I have received from the LORD was that people will move from one country to another to be able to complete their life lessons and He told me that we should not treat these people bad we should accept them as GOD is the one who has opened the gates for everyone who needs to enter our countries and no one can shut these gates because He is watching over all of us.

Another message I received was that GOD has removed the four Angels who were balancing the universe because the end of time is near and He is now taken over and no man has control anymore.

Yes it is true because when the LORD asked me to write the delayed book of laws, He did tell me to remind everyone about the end of time so that we can all prepare ourselves for His coming, and the LORD is now opening the words which are written on the scroll which was sealed by Daniel to us, and the LORD is working through the chosen people who will remind us about how to prepare ourselves.

All I am doing I am only writing what the LORD tells me to write. You must all remember that I am only a messenger and I get told by the LORD what to do and I only go according to the instructions. I have to send these messages to the world as I am being instructed by the LORD. If I do not send these messages I will only be delaying our spiritual growth.

It is up to an individual to work out what they believe. But I will do the will of GOD not the will of mankind. I have served humanity now I am serving GOD our Father as He chose me to work for Him. It did take a long time for me to understand what GOD was asking me to do, because I was lost in the world, but, GOD did not give up on me. He convinced me by sending people who confirmed to me that GOD was talking to me and also talked to me through visions and also healed people through me, and also wrote the book of messages through me. And these messages revealed what was written in the Bible. And these; messages do confirm the hidden secret of our spiritual journey. And these messages can be read from the book which is called:—LET US CELEBRATE THE END OF TIME AND DANCE TO THE MUSIC OF TIME= BY THANDI GEORGE.

After reading the book, you will be able to understand your journey and my journey and you will be able to understand why our LORD taught us to forgive.

LET US READ THE TEACHINGS OF JOHN SO THAT WE CAN TRY TO UNDERSTAND ONE OF THE MISTERYS OF LIFE AND THESE WILL TEACH US THAT WE ARE ALL HEAR ON EARTH TO FULFILL GOD'S PURPOSE AND TO LEARN THE LESSONS OF LIFE.

JOHN 9: 1-12

JESUS HEALS A MAN BORN BLIND

As JESUS went along, He saw a man blind from birth. His disciples asked Him, Rabbi, who sinned, this man or his parents, that he was born blind?

Neither this man nor his parents sinned, said JESUS.

BUT

THIS HAPPENED SO THAT THE WORK OF GOD MIGHT BE DISPLAYED IN HIS LIFE.

PLEASE TAKE NOTE

Everything which we go through in our lives is meant to be for our spiritual growth, it is not meant to hurt us; it means, we should be able to teach each other what is right and educate each other, not to do the wrong things which will delay our spiritual growth. All these laws have been written before, the laws which teach us what is wrong and what is right. This is why this book is written only to remind us of what is wrong and what is right because we have now reached the end of our lessons of life.

Each individual have learned all these lessons through life after life which they were given through reincarnation. Now the end of our lessons has come to its end, it is now time for revision.

And after revision it is time for judgement, believe it or not? The sings of the end are starting to show and we can all see them. There is no harm for us to change our ways and do what is good, because we all know that good deeds always bring good results and bad deeds will always ruin our lives and live us with guilt for life, so it does make sense to change our ways, because if we suffered pain in the earth world why should we suffer again in the next.

We have learned that our spirit lives forever and it evolves to a higher being. So; why don't we want to explore the next world which we are being told that!

There will be no pain, only happiness.

AND

There will be no hard work for a change.

AND

There will be no confusion at all?

Let us think carefully about this message; I can assure you, no one wants to suffer again and again.

"Who" wants to suffer on earth and again in hell?

Not **M**e!—I have experienced so much pain in this world, watching people destroy me and destroy a lot of innocent people, only—to fulfil their sinful needs, and I have watched, these people fading away like thin clouds, up to no existence. And I told myself I would rather be in my grave than destroy myself or destroy others. When I turned to the LORD and question the LORD about life He did answer me.

There were times when I thought I will never find answers about life; as I thought that the LORD did not hear my prayers. I was wrong, the LORD did hear my prayers and He was ready to answer them at the right time, and He was preparing the Angels who will guide me and He wanted me to see that there are lots of things which happen in the world which we all have to learn and we can never evolve if we do not know what is wrong and put it right. Only the LORD can open our eyes to see the light and understand the secret of life, which will lead us to our purpose.

JOHN 9: 4-5

JESUS CHRIST says to us; As long as it is day, we must do the work of Him who sent Him because night is coming, when no—one can work.

Then:—JESUS CHRIST carried on and said. WHILE I AM IN THE WORLD, I AM THE LIGHT OF THE WORLD.

Yes! Our LORD JESUS anointed me with His light, because I asked him to. And now I have found my way back home and I have learned sharing the light of GOD with all GOD'S children, and GOD'S creation.

What I went through in my life was learning the lessons of life so that I can be able to share my story with others who are learning the same lessons and those who will be learning the same lessons in the future and those who are learning other lesson, to be able to comfort them on their spiritual journey, and help them to understand that we are all here to learn from each other. And to teach others that; we all experience Pain and Happiness now and again and we will always experience Birth and Death, it is how it is, and it will be like that until the end of time, because it is for the good us all mainly for our spiritual purpose.

ALL I am looking forward:— is to see the Holy Land which GOD promised us. I know that there is more to life than we all know, and I am not the only one who knows this, because I have met the children of GOD in this world and these children of GOD are around us, and they are teaching us, about our spiritual journey but; we ignore them because we are frightened of our selves.

Now that I have experienced the light of GOD which was always in me, and this light was blocked by the lessons of life, I feel free and I have learned to love myself and to love everyone and to love all GOD's creation; because, I know that GOD loves us and I can never blame GOD for man's evil deeds anymore, I know that when GOD created the world GOD created the world with love and gave us all kinds of food and everything we needed to keep us healthy and strong while we are learning the lessons of life, but all what was suppose—to keep me strong, was taken by the greedy people who only thought about themselves not others. I know that GOD loves us, and I now know that GOD has a purpose for all of us.

And I know that our LORD JESUS CHRIST died on the cross for us because we failed to listen to what He was teaching us and we still fail to listen even today and we keep on making mistake after mistake even when we see the truth. I am one of those who will follow the LORD'S teachings and teach according to what the LORD instructs me to teach.

AND

I will hold on to the cross until the end of time, which is not too far, but, very close. Why don't you start holding tight on the cross and never let it slip, because you are the only who is accountable for your own deeds, at the end, no one will be there with you, you will be alone on the day of judgement. Just like at the end of the day, you have to find your way home, it is the same with our spirit, our, spirit is longing for home.

Why do we not want to believe in the teaching of the prophets of GOD and the teachings of our LORD JESUS CHRIST?

And

Why do we think we know everything when we do not even understand ourselves?

And

Why? Doctors are still not able to cure some illnesses? And bring our lives back or save our lives, because GOD our creator is the only one who knows our time to be born and our time to live the world and He is the only one who gives life and He is the only one who sets examples. Doctors can only work with the body but not the spirit because GOD is spirit, and we are spirits, the body is for earth the spirit is for Heaven.

And

This is why GOD sent prophets to us so they can teach us about the spirit and to show the mystery of GOD by healing those who Doctors cannot heal so that we can know that there is GOD and He is our Creator our Father, this is why now and again GOD sends us prophets who are around us, now, at this moment and are able to cure what the doctor's failed to heal.

And

What I do not understand is:—Why do we fight for what we call our country's which we can't even take with us to the grave when we die.

And

Why do we think that one race is more intelligent, than another?

Why do we think we know better than the creator Himself?

PLEASE Think Carefully, how can someone know your creation better than you the creator who created it?

We all know that we can't steal anyone's creation and make it ours, all we will end up with, is guilt and fear of being caught and taken to prison or being charged for what we have stolen.

Now it is the time to search for the creator who created us with love.

And

Learn about creation and question our Creator by prayer and by reading books which will give us wisdom.

And

Learn to talk to people who are questioning life.

And

This will bring us closer to who we are, and not what people tell us.

And

Not what people tell us about what the world is?

And

Teach us about how to oppress people around us?

And

Teach us **h**ow take advantage of the poor so that we can fulfil our desires.

All these desires which lead us to oppress others, these are called evil desires.

AND

If our desires are uncontrollable, we have to work hard to fulfil these desires without oppressing people who work hard for us. We must treat these people with love, because without them we cannot reach our goals.

Life means working together with love and respect for others. It is what we call team work.

This message is only to teach us about, how to live a good life and do the right thing. At the end of the day everyone has a choice of how to live their lives, but we must remember that humanity still stands, as we do not want to be unfairly treated you as well do not want us to treat you unfairly.

Make me an image of you.

AND

Let me make you an image of me.

AS

We are already the image of GOD.

And

GOD created us in **His own image because GOD loved** us.

We are one with each other and this is why we should not hurt each other, because, GOD did not hurt us because GOD can't hurt Himself and you cannot hurt yourself, you and me can only love like our Father loves.

I can only remind you and me that there is more to life than we know. And there are mysteries which are happening around us every minute and we do not see them because we think we know better than the Creator of all. We can never know better than our Creator we will only be fooling ourselves and people around us, but we cannot fool GOD.

To be able to understand life we all have to believe the one, who came from Heaven and taught us that, there is more than we know about life; and He told us that He will be going back to where He came from, and He did go back where He came from which is where we came from and His prophesy was fulfilled, and that person was the son of GOD who is JESUS CHRIST.

He performed miracles and healed people and taught us how to live a perfect life and He confirmed all what was to come, and, what to come is now and again becoming fruitful. But; some people pretend they do not see because they carry so much anger inside themselves.

They are angry with GOD and blaming GOD for human error.

And

They are blaming GOD for their mistakes which they failed to recognise.

So!—It has become a big thing for blaming GOD so that we can receive mercy from others by telling our stories of why:—We damage our bodies with alcohol

And

Why we kill our brains by taking drugs which destroy us and people who care for us.

And

Why we do not get the jobs we want.

And

Why our countries are in a mess.

And

Why someone we love died of a certain disease, or a certain accident.

And

Other misfortunes which occurs to us, now and again!

It is our duty as individuals; to search for the truth about life than destroying ourselves and people around us. The religious books are written to teach us about what is the right thing to do. You are not the only one going through pain. We are all experiencing some kind of pain now and again, but we do our best to have courage to move on without blaming GOD.

PLEASE THINK CAREFULLY

What if there is no GOD? **W**ho will you blame?

YES!

You; will blame the person who hurt you, because you know the person who hurt you, and that is the person who is guilty for hurting you.

You will not point a finger at someone you do not know and blame them for hurting you. So now let us face the facts; GOD did not hurt you, someone you know very well is hurting you and you know who it is, and you are protecting them or you are the one who put yourself in a certain situation which led to your anger and your misery.

Now that you have learned that GOD or no GOD, you are responsible for every action you take and the consequences are yours to endure. Because we are all sailing in the same boat called Earth and if this boat sinks you are the one to save yourself.

Well' now let's get back to ourselves and do the right thing and let us not become slaves to the world, and slaves to our perpetrators.

I was the same before when I blamed GOD for everything which happened to me I even blamed GOD for giving me an abusive husband. Now I have learned that it was my choice, and GOD our loving Father was not there when I chose this man amongst so many, but, this is the man I loved very much, and no one could have stopped me from marrying this man, I made a bad choice because I thought he was a loving and steady man but, he was a miserable man who was angry with GOD.

Even me his wife I could not convince this man that there is GOD so I fell in the same trap and I started to believe that GOD is the one who is giving power to my abusive husband to physically abuse me and mentally abuse me and I stared to believe that GOD is allowing all this abuse, but, even though I was angry with GOD, deep inside me I knew that GOD or there is no GOD. The must be more to life than we know.

I kept on praying as I was told to pray and never gave up praying, at the end—GOD removed me from this man and healed me. When GOD finished healing He sent His son our LORD JESUS CHRIST to come and bless me. And after blessing me I asked our LORD never to leave me again, and I allowed my LORD to work through me. And I discarded the earthly things and emptied myself to work for the LORD I will never work for the world again. I will work for the LORD, because the world burned me alive.

The choices we make are our choices we cannot blame GOD or people around us or our parents, because the teachings of the laws are written everywhere.

I do admit that some children have made wrong choices because of the people who bring them up, but when they become older they do automatically know what is wrong and what is right because we are all born with the knowledge of being able to differentiate between both, and it is the gift from GOD to us.

After receiving the light of GOD and understanding the ways of GOD and reading the teachings of the prophets and the teachings of our LORD JESUS CHRIST and the teachings of all religions I found more light to the meaning of life the more I searched the more I found. And now I am one with all.

And I learned that by choosing the husband I chose helped to search for GOD and found that Home and comfort which my spirit was searching for and longing for, so I do thank my Husband for directing me home back to my Father who is GOD our Father.

Now I have found my Father I cannot hate anyone, I can only forgive and love, but I do move away from those who hurt me so that I cannot forget GOD my Father again. I still do love my husband but, I can never live with Him, because he is still searching and he is the only one who can search and find his purpose and fulfil it, I cannot help him, and he is the one who will learn his lessons of life.

This is one of the mysteries of life which most of us do not understand. Which is; everything which happens around us leads us somewhere higher that we know. All we need to do is—to pray for directions and we will find the way.

WE ARE NOT RESPONSIBLE

FOR

OUR HUSBANDS FAILURE'S!

AND

THE HUSBAND IS ALSO NOT RESPONSIBLE

FOR

HIS WIFES FAILURE'S!

And

WE ARE NOT RESPONSIBLE

FOR

OUR CHILDRENS FAILURE'S!

"BUT"

WE MUST TEACH OUR CHILDREN HOW TO LIVE A GOOD FULFILLING LIFE AND TEACH THEM ONLY WHAT IS GOOD. AND TEACH THEM ABOUT GOD OUR CREATOR. THIS WILL HELP OUR CHILDREN FROM DOING EVIL TO OTHERS.

WE ARE NOT RESPONSIBLE

FOR

ANYONE'S FAILURE'S!

WE ARE RESPONSIBLE FOR OUR OWN FAILURE'S!

AND

WE WILL BE HELD ACCOUNTABLE FOR OUR DEEDS!

JUST

AS IT IS ON EARTH IT WILL BE THE SAME AT THE END!

WE CAN NEVER BE LEFT UNPUNISHED FOR THE EVIL DEED'S—WE CAUSED TO OTHERS

GOD OUR FATHER CANNOT BE CHEATED

HE SEES BEYOND WHERE NO EYE CAN SEE. HE OPENS THE EYES OF THOSE WHO READY TO SEE BEYOND.

GOD is a loving GOD, and He still does everything to help us understand life.

We are the ones who live in sin, and fail to hear the voice of GOD our Father.

We are the ones who kill each other.

We are the ones who destroy each other.

We are the ones who hate each other.

If only we can do the right thing, we will be better people and we will live in a better world, but, we <u>bring up generations of people who are confused and live</u> in fear and embracing guilt.

Instead <u>of living in love, and embracing love.</u>

And

Instead <u>of caring for each other we destroy each other.</u>

And

INSTEAD <u>of teaching our children to love we teach them to hate others.</u> We instil fear instead of courage.

And that has never brought any happiness to us at all.

Now that we have made all these mistakes and the world is in a mess. All we can do now; is each individual to find the truth about who they are, and what is their purpose on earth? So, that we do not get brainwashed by others anymore. Then we will learn to accept our mistakes and put them right and we will learn that the Bible tells us that we are accountable for our own deeds not others.

Let us gain wisdom and discard evil.

And

Let us love and care for each other.

FOR

It is time for the End

As

There was **T**ime for the **B**eginning.

Now

Let us prepare ourselves, for the coming of the LORD.

And

Let us listen to the LORD and live according to His teachings.

And

Let us not be the children of the Devil.

JOHN 8:42-47

JESUS said to the people who were listening to Him; If, GOD were your Father, you would love me, for I came from GOD and now am here. I came on my own; but he sent me. Why is my language not clear to you, because you are unable to hear what I say?

You belong to your Father the devil, and you want to carry out your Father's desire. He was a murderer from the beginning not holding to the truth, for there is no truth in him. When he lies, he speaks his native language, for he is a liar, and the father of lies.

Yet because I tell you the truth, you do not believe me! Can any of you prove me guilty of sin? If I am telling the truth, why don't you believe me?

HE WHO BELONGS TO GOD **H**EARS—**W**HAT GOD SAYS

THE REASON YOU DO NOT HEAR

"IS"

THAT YOU DO NOT BELONG TO GOD

PLEASE TAKE NOTE

THERE IS TIME FOR EVERYTHING

AND

THIS TIME **I**S—TIME TO CHANGE

ECCELESTIASIS3:1-8

There is time for everything, and a season for every **activity under Heaven.**

(1) A TIME TO BE BORN AND A TIME TO DIE.

These times are meant to be, mainly for our spiritual growth.

A time to be born was the time when GOD created the world. And when GOD created the world He wanted us to be able to serve each other with love and He also wanted us to learn the lessons of life, so that we can be pure, and be able to go back home to Heaven. And He also sent Angels to guide us and the prophets to teach us about the true ways we should live so that we can be able to go back home to the father. At the beginning we did not understand the laws and we kept on sinning. And because we kept on sinning GOD our Father realised that we have sinned, He decided to ask Moses to write the laws for us.

And these are the laws which our Father has taught us, as He asked Moses to teach us about these laws which we should practise. Because GOD knew that we will have to learn these lessons to be able to discard evil.

We will start with the TEN COMMANDMENTS THE TEN COMMANDMENTS

EXODUS20: I-17

[1] And GOD spoke all these words:

[2] I am the LORD your GOD, who brought you out of Egypt, out of the land of slavery.

[3] "You shall have no other god's before me.

[4] "You shall not make yourself an idol in any in the form of anything in heaven above or on earth beneath or in the water's below.

[5] "You shall not bow down to them or worship them; for I, the LORD your GOD, am a jealous GOD, punishing the children for the sin of their father's to the third and fourth generation of those who hate me.

[6] But showing love to a thousand {generations} of those who love me and keep my commandments.

[7] You must not misuse the name of the LORD your GOD, for the LORD will not hold anyone guiltless who misuses his name.

[8] "Remember on the Sabbath day by keeping it holy.

[9] Six days you shall labour and do all your work.

[10] But the seventh day is a Sabbath to the LORD your GOD. On it you shall not do any work, neither you, nor your son or daughter nor your man servant or maid servant, nor your animals, nor the alien within your gates.

[11] For in six days the LORD made the heavens and the earth, the sea, and all that is in them, but He rested on the seventh day. Therefore the LORD blessed the Sabbath day and made it Holy.

[12] "Honour your father and your mother, so that you may live long in the land the LORD your GOD is giving you.

[13] "You shall not murder.

[14] "You shall not commit adultery.

[15] "You shall not steal

[16] "**Y**ou shall not give false testimony against your neighbour.

[17] "**Y**ou shall not covet your neighbour's house. You shall not covet you neighbour's wife, or his manservant, or maidservant, his ox or donkey or anything that belongs to your neighbour.

PLEASE NOTE

Neighbour does not only mean your next door neighbour it also means your fellow citizen nationwide and worldwide.

These commandments are very important to all of us. This is why the world went wrong, because we did not live according to these laws of GOD.

There are more laws which Moses had written for us, it will be wise for us to start looking through the bible and read these laws, and keep up to Moses teachings. One of the most important part of the body which always sins is the tongue. We must always be careful at what we say to others.

PROVERBS 18:21

The tongue has the power

Of

Life and death

The words in this book are the healing words they are meant to build lives and not to destroy lives.

MESSAGES WHICH I RECEIVED

FROM

THE LORD JESUS CHRIST

When the LORD started talking to me He told me that I will have to confirm what is written in the bible, So that we can remember the teachings of the prophets.

Then He said to tell everyone the following messages.

[1] To detach from Earthly things, which; means we must start searching for our life purpose.

[2] To read the story of JOB in the bible; which will give us faith in GOD and courage to move on.

[3] To build places of worship, which; means we must give ourselves time to pray.

[4] We must carry our sword on our backs, which; means we must stop wars and stop killing each other, and live in peace with each other.

[5] We must read the story of Daniel, in the Bible. Which will decrease our fear.

[6] We must read the book of Exodus and the Revelations; which will help us to understand the beginning and the end.

[7] We must embrace all Religions because they all come from GOD and they worship the same GOD.

OTHER MESSAGES

[1] To remind us that there is a book of life, which; is the book each individual receives when they are born, this is where everything is written for us about which time we will be learning certain lessons of life and the time we will learn these lessons and the time we will finish these lessons and the time we will discard our bodies to have a rest so that we can come back to learn other lessons. And this works through reincarnation.

[2] To remind us that there is also a Book That Is life. This book is the book which GOD awards us with our spiritual gifs every time we finish the lesson which we were learning on earth.

And each achieved lesson receives a spiritual gift from GOD, and this is what the prophets tells us that we must keep our gifts in Heaven where thieves cannot steal them and moth will not destroy them.

WHAT ARE SPIRITUAL GIFTS?

[3] Spiritual Gifts are gifts which we receive from GOD our Father, these gifts are kept in Heaven, but, now and again GOD our Father will send us a sign in our dreams or vision or a mystery to tell us that we have received a spiritual gift from him, but because we do not understand the ways of GOD we fail to recognise these gifts we talk about our dreams and miracles which occurred, or visions we have seen, not realising that GOD has awarded us with our spiritual gifts.

Now is the time for the anointment as our LORD said He will come and anoint His chosen children. It is true I have met the anointed children of GOD who told me about mysteries which occurred and wonderful dreams which they dreamt and some of them told me that they have experience seeing a huge beam of light and when they tried to point out to the people sitting next to them it did not work because these people said they could not see the beam of light.

And

Some people have told me that they had dreams receiving flowers mainly red roses.

And

Some people told me that they received bundles of different flowers.

And

Some received visions of Angels and they talk about how comforting it was to see the Angels of our LORD coming to visit them and talking to them.

And

Some people have come across people who prayed for them and they felt spiritually healed and all their problems came to an end and they received happiness again which they lost long time ago and they feel they have just experienced a re-birth.

And

Some people have experienced a mystery voice talking to them and giving messages of comfort and warnings about the future.

These are what we call spiritual gift's, we all have received some kind of spiritual gifts now and again in this life and in our past lives. Only GOD can offer these gifts. No man can offer spiritual gifts because these gifts are kept in the BOOK THAT IS LIFE.

WHAT ARE EARTHLY GIFTS?

Man can only offer the gifts of Earth and these gifts don't last long and we can't take them with us when we die.

To be able to receive our spiritual gifts is to be able to keep to the good laws of the teaching of the prophets of all religions.

When virtuous mysteries, visions, miracles happen to you, and people around you tell you that you are being deceived by the devil, do not believe them, the devil cannot deceive anymore using righteousness, and if they want to convince you that you are crazy, just ignore them they do not understand the ways of the LORD. And do not be afraid, keep on praying for directions.

You are the one who knows the truth about yourself and only GOD who knows the truth about you, so rejoice because GOD is talking to you and our LORD is anointing you, you are one of the chosen ones. This is time for the END OF THE WORLD. The scripture is being fulfilled.

MAY THE LOVE OF GOD BE WITH ALL GOD'S CHILDREN

THE END OF TIME

ACTS 1:1-11

JESUS CHRIST TAKEN UP TO HEAVEN

This is the message from the servant of GOD. He says, in—his former book, Theophilus; I wrote about all that JESUS began to do and to teach until the day He was taken up to Heaven, after giving instructions through the Holy Spirit to the apostles He had chosen.

After his suffering, he showed himself to these men and gave many convincing proofs that He was alive. He appeared to them over a period of forty days and spoke about the Kingdom of GOD.

On one occasion, while He was eating with them, he gave them His command: Do not leave Jerusalem, but, wait for the gift my father promised, which you have heard me speak about.

For John Baptised with water, but in a few days you will be baptised with Holy Spirit.

So when they met me together, they asked him. LORD are you at this time going to restore the Kingdom to Israel?

He said to them it is not for you to know the times or dates the Father has set by His own authority. But you will receive power when the Holy Spirit comes on you; and you will be witnesses in Jerusalem, and in all Judea and Samaria, and to the ends of the world.

After He said this, He was taken up before their very eyes and a cloud hid Him from their sight.

They were looking intently up, into the sky as He was going, when suddenly two men dressed in white stood beside them. Men of Galilee,—they said—why do you stand here and looking into the sky? This same JESUS, who has been taken from you into Heaven, will come back in the same way you have seen him go into Heaven.

PLEASE TAKE NOTE

Well it is true Jesus is coming soon, He did say when the Holy Spirit comes there will be witnesses in Jerusalem and all Judea and Samaria, and to the Ends Of The world.

This delayed book of messages you are reading right now confirms the coming of JESUS CHRIST and He is the one who is writing these messages through me. In one of the messages I have received from the LORD was that there will be eighteen books written by different authors and we must look for them and read them. Each book will be published in different languages and at the right time and these books will be directed by the LORD Himself.

THERE IS TIME FOR EVRYTHING

A TIME **T**O **P**LANT

AND

A TIME **T**O **U**PROOT

When Adam and Eve ate the forbidden fruit, it was time to plant good and bad thoughts in our minds so that we can be able to tell the difference between both. This is why the snake told Eve that she should eat the fruit which GOD forbid man to eat in the Garden of Eden. GOD knew that the snake will deceive the woman and the woman will encourage the man to do the wrong thing. Even though GOD knew that this will happen, GOD knew that man should be taught both good and bad, that is why GOD had to teach us through this method to make man known to him.

By punishing the woman GOD is only teaching us that if we do not listen, we will get into trouble and we will only hurt ourselves, these teachings are good teachings to us. Just like; when we teach our little ones not to hurt themselves, So, GOD does not mean to hurt us but to teach us.

Since then the women was punished with the pains of giving labour.

The man was punished with painful toil.

AND

The snake was punished by being cursed for life by GOD for deceiving the woman.

That was the time to learn good and evil, and now it is time for us to receive our award for doing the right thing and to show GOD that we have learned our lessons, because this is the end of time, if anyone is still struggling to understand what is good and what is bad. All you need to do is to look at Moses commandments and do the right thing.

WHAT EVIL HAVE WE LEARNED
NOT
TO PRACTICE

GENESIS 2:15-17

The LORD GOD took the man and put him in the Garden of Eden to work it and take care of it. And the lord GOD commanded the man. You are free to eat from any tree in the Garden; but you must not eat from the tree of the knowledge of good and evil.

GENESIS 3: 1-5

Now the serpent was more, crafty than any of the wild animals that the LORD GOD had made. He said to the woman. Did GOD really say, you must not eat from any tree in the Garden!

The woman said to the serpent, we may eat fruit from the trees in the garden, but, GOD did say. You must not eat the fruit from the tree which is in the middle of the Garden, and you must not touch it, or you will die.

You will not surely die, the serpent said to the woman, for GOD knows that when you eat of it, your eyes will be opened, and you be like GOD, knowing good and evil.

This reading from Geneses brings us back to our teaching of time. It was time for learning to differentiate between good and evil.

What are the evil things we were told by Moses not to do?

EXODUS 20:4-6

You shall not make for yourself an idol in the form of anything in heaven above or on earth beneath or in the waters below.

You shall not bow down to them or worship them, for I the LORD your GOD am a jealous GOD, punishing the children for the sin of their Father's to the third and fourth generation of those who hate me, but showing love to a thousand generations of those who love me and keep my commandments.

What is our biggest mistake?

Which

We all did on Earth?

[1] **A**t the begging of life we made Idols and worshipped them, the bible tells us in that in the past people made their own gods and worshipped them. That made GOD very angry. But then man learned that it was wrong to worship man made gods.

[2] **W**e are now worshipping our leaders and making them our GOD, because we believe that they will change our lives and give us whatever we want, forgetting that they also have to serve us with love. Instead; of us killing each other, for the leaders who are also searching for the meaning of life. We must turn and search for GOD'S purpose.

This is the biggest mistake we are doing now. We are treating our leaders as our GOD. And they are unable to provide all each individual needs we become angry with each other and blame each other and bring up confused children in this world.

This is why GOD says He will punish all those who do not worship him because GOD is the one who created us He is the only one who can lead us. Our leaders should lead according to the teachings of GOD, then we will be happy because we will all be able to hear the voice of GOD, and follow GOD'S directions, because every leader we choose was also chosen by GOD himself who knows His ways of doing things and GOD who knows what our needs are, but we are so impatient that now and again out of anger we kill each other and kill our leaders. Because, we have made these leaders our gods!

If we can pray and ask GOD to lead us we will not be depressed we will be able to humble ourselves and be able to pray for our leaders to find the truth about what they should do to make us happy.

There is no leader who will be able to fulfil all our needs, because we all have different needs and it is impossible to focus on each individual needs. And the country to be run properly also has its needs. So we will all learn that we can't depend on our leaders to provide all our needs.

BUT

Our leaders now should stop provoking war which teaches us to kill. They must now throw away the weapons of war away. This will help us to find our spiritual journey and to be able to finish some of the lessons of life which we have not finish learning; because now it is time to uproot, and the time to learn evil has now come to an end. ALL human beings are now searching their way back to the Father and the LORD is ready to open the doors of Heaven as He has promised.

THIS IS THE
MESSAGE TO THE LEADER'S

THE LORD ASKED ME TO RIGHT THIS MESSAGE

[1] Every ruler must rule with love

[2] Every ruler must give shelter to his people, and divide land accordingly, because, every living being deserves respect and privacy.

[3] Every ruler must now stop wars and throw away the weapons and use the money to help the people in need and this will also help to stop pain to the innocent people who do not believe in war, and are trying to find their spiritual journey.

[4] Every ruler must make sure that there is enough food for everyone by supporting charities which provides the poor with food and clothing.

[5] Every ruler must make sure that they rule with love, and they must not discriminate amongst the rich and the poor.

[6] Every ruler must learn the teachings of religion so that they can learn how to serve humanity with love, because now it is time to uproot.

[7] Every ruler must make sure that the oppressor to be locked up in prison, and the evil people should be locked up in prison, and the persecutors to do their jobs without taking bribes.

[8] Every ruler must make sure the people of the law are serving humanity with love, and they are not suppose, to accept bribes to protect the guilty.

[9] Every ruler must make sure that he does not discriminate against colour, gender, and [alien's] foreigner's because, we are all foreigner's in this world and GOD put us in this world to come and learn the lessons of life and also to learn from each other. Time of separation has come to an end. The lessons of life are now being learned it is time to embrace each other with love.

This is what serving humanity with love means.

It means equal rights for all and Love for all, because GOD does not believe in favouritism. GOD created us with Love.

HOW WILL GOD PUNISH
THE
LEADERS WHO OPPRESS THEIR PEOPLE?

JAMES 2 :8-12

If you really keep the royal law found in scripture, love your neighbour as yourself, you are doing right—BUT—If you show favouritism, you sin and are convicted by the law as law-breakers.

FOR

Whoever keeps the whole law and yet stumbles at just one point is guilty of breaking all of it.

JAMES 2:12

Speak and act as those who are going to be judged by the law that gives freedom, because judgement without mercy will be shown to anyone who has not been merciful.

MERCY TRIUMPHS OVER JUDGEMENT

HEBREWS 12-14

Make sure every effort to live in peace with all men and be Holy; without holiness no-one misses the grace of GOD and that no-one will see the LORD.

See to it that no-one misses the Grace of GOD and that no bitter root grows up to defile many.

PLEASE TAKE NOTE

Now we have learned how our leaders should provide for us, so that we can all enjoy the grace of GOD.

We also understand that at the beginning of life we were still in the dark when we worshipped idols and then GOD put the laws for us, through Moses to teach us that we must only worship GOD. Now we do not have an excuse that we do not know what the law says.

LET'S START WORSHIPPING GOD

WORSHIPPING GOD OUR FATHER ONLY MEANS THAT; WE MUST NOW THROW AWAY THE PAST AND START RESPECTING EACH OTHER.

AND

START WORKING TOGETHER

AND

WE MUST START LOVING EACH OTHER.

THAT'S IT . . . . FULL STOP . . . .

AND

IT IS AS EASY AS . . . . A . . . . B . . . . C . . . .

It is easy as A. B. C. because there is time for everything and time gives us time to re-organise our lives.

A TIME TO KILL
AND
A TIME TO HEAL

Now; that we have spent our lives killing each other, for nothing at all. When we look back we will realise how stupid the whole thing was, because we did not achieve anything after that, and our children are still carrying on with the same evil, of believing that we should kill each other to be able to achieve whatever we want to achieve. Yes at that time it did seem right to kill each other and bow down to our Kings and make fools of our selves because we were learning the lessons OF LIFE.

Now that we know that killing each other does not pay, all it does it brings unhappiness to all of us. And those who have instructed us to kill are all sitting happily in their homes enjoying all sorts of luxuries, while, the soldiers of war are, living with the guilt of murder and confused about the world and its purpose and while the soldier has nothing, to eat and nothing to feed their families.

That was the time to learn the lesson of what happens when we kill each other. Because this is what happens when we kill each other; we will pay for doing evil and we will be left desolate by those who instructed us to do evil and that is the lesson we have learned, and now it is the time to put it right, because there is no time anymore to sit and pretend that killing brings us joy or killing will bring us pride, and also that killing will keep away foreign people in what we call our Countries. And that killing will help us take our countries to the grave with us so that we can protect our countries from the intruders.

No! We all die and live our countries behind for other people to enjoy what we have left behind for them, just like those who were before us, they left us knowledge so that we can upgrade from what they left for us. Now we have to do the same and make it better for others instead of destroying what has been created with love for us. We are not living in the days of Noah we are the people of knowledge we now know; what is right and what is bad.

Gone are those days of learning the lesson of killing. We also have learned that killing people for their money which they have worked hard for; does not help at all, because we have watched people ending up in prison for this crime and we have watched how their families suffer for enjoying blood money.

Yes! It was time for those who were learning that lesson.

Now it is time for all of us to forgive each other and heal the world. The—do not kill lesson has been learnt and those who still think of practising that kind of lesson I am afraid time is over.

It is now time to move on and find your purpose and fulfil it.

It is now time for you to teach those who are in prisons for committing the crime and teach them that you have been there and it did not do you any good. It was just a waste of a precious life you have taken away from someone. And now you are awaiting judgement from GOD our Father and if you do that GOD will forgive your sins. Because at the time you were in the dark now you are in the light.

It is now time to heal each other, because now we are reaching the end of our lessons. There is no more to pretend that we do not know what Moses has taught us in the book of GENESIS about GOD'S Commandments to man, and the teachings of the prophets.

2 CORINTHIANS 1:8-9

We do not want you to be uninformed, brothers about the hardships we suffered in the province of Asia. We were under great pressure, far beyond our ability to endure, so that we even despaired even of life.

Indeed, in our hearts we felt the sentence of death, but this happened that we must not rely on ourselves, but on GOD, who raises the dead.

PLASE TAKE NOTE

This time is time for healing each other.

A TIME TO TEAR DOWN

AND
A TIME TO BUILD

Now that we have destroyed the world and brought so much poverty, racism, discrimination, depression, confusion, hatred and so much anger and destroyed our planet which we can't put right even if we tried; the only thing left for us is to turn to the teaching of GOD and ask him for a solution.

[1] We have killed the innocent people.

[2] We have destroyed nature.

[3] We have polluted the sea.

[4] We have polluted the rivers.

[5]We have destroyed countries.

[6] We have oppressed the poor.

[7]We have taken from the good people.

All these did not help at all, because our freedom of life is being taken away from us.

The rich live behind locked bars like prisoners.

AND

The poor live behind locked bars, just like prisoners.

What is the difference between the poor person and the rich person when they both live in fear? What is the purpose of life for both, and where is their freedom?

All I see; is that the rich can still eat what They want and the poor still has to beg. Then what is life without the freedom to live it and enjoy it. Both poor and rich need spiritual freedom, freedom to live again. And that could only be found by forgiving each other, and move on to find their spiritual journey, then; they will both receive the freedom of the spirit which will bring happiness to both.

Because now we have learned our lesson of tearing down, which helped us to destroy our beautiful planet and after destroying our planet we have now gained fear of losing our lives, because whatever happens to the planet both rich and poor will be affected. If our planet has to kill us, we will all die.

What we can do to try and make this earth comfortable and enjoy our last days on this earth it is for each individual to search for their purpose and fulfil their purpose and this will lead to serving humanity with love, which was what it was meant to be from the beginning when Moses wrote the commandments of how to live a perfect life.

Now that we have made a mess, let us now make it the time to re—build our own lives,

Because

We cannot re-build the world

And

We cannot remove the locked bars which we have put on our doors.

And

We cannot get our freedom of life back.

We did all this evil to innocent people and taken from poor countries and destroyed their countries and killed these innocent children of GOD because of greed, now we are left behind locked bars and imprisoned ourselves and we can never be free anymore this means we will always live in fear and guilt.

That was time to tear down, and now it is time to re-build.

WHAT DID WE DO TO IMPRISON OURSELVES?

EXODUS 20: 13

YOU SHALL NOT MURDER!

EXODUS 20: 15

YOU SHALL NOT STEAL

We have murdered the poor and stolen from them, this is why we have imprisoned ourselves.

We will never escape this prison this is why there is so much security needed these days, everywhere we go, we are being watched whether good or bad.

A TIME TO WEEP
AND
A TIME TO LAUGH

Now that we have experienced prison and we are all locked up in our prison cells, and we have found out what has locked us in these cells.

It is time for us to step back and help our victims and give them education so that, they can also find their spiritual journey and fulfil it. And GOD will forgive our sins. And GOD will unlock our cells and we will be spiritually free, and that is what our spirit is searching for.

Our spirit is searching for:—Not the Earthly riches—BUT—The spiritual riches!

<u>Let this time—Be our time to laugh.</u>

FOR, SO IN ADAM ALL SHAL DIE

AND

FOR IN CHRIST ALL WILL BE MADE ALIVE

THIS IS TIME TO CELEBRATE THE COMING OF THE LORD—LET US MAKE THIS TIME THE TIME TO LAUGH!

A TIME TO MOURN

AND
A TIME TO DANCE

Once we have mourned our grief and found our spiritual journey we will all be happy and we will be able to live with each other happily and we will be able to trust each other. The locked bars will still be there; but, our spirit would be free.

There is no time to mourn anymore our time is limited it is time to enjoy our last days on earth. We must change our ways and forgive other's and forgive ourselves and **DANCE TO THE MUSIC OF TODAY.**

Planet Earth was a wonderful teacher full of bearable thorns. Now let's thank Planet earth, and give Him our last warmest greetings.

REVELATIONS22: 12-

Behold I am coming soon! **My** reward is with me, and I will give to everyone according to what they have done.

I am the **A**lpha and The **O**mega

The First And The Last!

PLEASE TAKE NOTE

Now:—have a bit of homework to workout which time can help you to find your spiritual journey as the end of the world is starting to come like a thief to steal our lives. Read and see what you can change to make your life better and bring your happiness back.

ECCELESSIASTES 3: 5-8

A TIME TO SCATTER STONES AND
A TIME TO GATHER THEM

A TIME TO EMBRACE AND A TIME

TO REFRAIN

A TIME TO SEARCH AND A TIME

TO GIVE UP

A TIME TO KEEP A TIME

TO THROW AWAY

A TIME TO TEAR AND A TIME TO MEND

A TIME TO BE SILENT AND A TIME

TO SPEAK

A TIME TO LOVE AND A TIME TO HATE

A TIME FOR WAR AND A TIME

FOR PEACE

Yes we are all striving for peace.

PEACE BE WITH ALL THE CHILDREN OF GOD

I HAVE CHOSEN THE TIME TO CELEBRATE THE END TIME

PROVEBS 29:18

Where there is no revelation, the people cast off restraint; but blessed is he who keeps the law.

HEBREWS 13: 1-3

Keep on loving each other as brothers! Do not forget to entertain strangers, for by so doing, some people have entertained angels without knowing it.

<u>HEBREWS 12: 5-6</u>

My son do not make light of the LORD'S DISCIPLES

AND

Do not lose heart when He rebukes you,

BECAUSE

The LORD disciplines those He loves,

AND

Punishes everyone He accepts as a son.

<u>2 CORINTHANS 6: 14-18</u>

Do not be yoked with unbelievers!

Do not be yoked together with unbelievers. For what do the righteousness and the wickedness have in common?

OR

What fellowship can light have with darkness?

What

Harmony is there between CHRIST and Belial?

What

Does a believer have with an unbeliever?

WHAT

Agreement is there—Between—The temple of GOD, and idols.

For

We are the temple of the living GOD

AS GOD HAS SAID

I will live with them and walk among them—And—I will be their GOD!

And they will be my Children.

Therefore come out from them and be separate—Says the LORD!

Touch no unclean thing and I will receive you.

I will be a Father to you and you will be my Sons and Daughters

SAYS THE LORD

We are the sons and daughters of GOD who were sent to earth to learn the lessons of life

JAMES 5:19-20

My Brothers, if one of you should wonder from the truth and someone brings him back, remember this. Whoever turns a sinner from the error of his way, will save him from death and cover a multitude of sins.

JAMES 5: 13-16

THE PRAYER OF FAITH

Is anyone of you in trouble—He should pray

Is anyone happy—Let him sing song of praise

Is anyone of you sick—He should call the Elders of the church to pray over him and anoint him with oil in the name of the LORD.

And the prayer offered in faith will make the sick person well; the LORD will raise him up.

If he has sinned he will be forgiven. Therefore confess your sins to each other and pray for each other so that you may be healed. The prayer of a righteous man is powerful and effective.

Elijah was a man just like us. He prayed earnestly that it world not rain, and it did not rain on the land for three and a half years. Again he prayed, and the Heavens gave rain, and the earth produced its crops.

PLEASE TAKE NOTE

MESSAGE TO ALL

I have now covered quite a few good readings from the Bible so that we can all be able to remember who we are and what we should do to be to be able to see the kingdom of Heaven. I hope this will help us to find our purpose in life and also help us to understand our pain and sorrows, and to be able to accept what is happening to us and how to handle these painful situations which come pass our lives without giving a warning and leave us confused and sad.

MAY THE LOVE OF GOD BE WITH ALL GOD'S CHILDREN

PART [6]

LEARNING TO RECOGNISE THE SIGNS OF THE END OF TIME TO BE ABLE TO—EMBRACE THE END OF TIME.

Part six [6] is to help us remember what the Bible taught us about how to recognise the signs of the end of time, so that we can start preparing ourselves. And also to remember the promises which our LORD JESUS said He will fulfil.

The signs of the end of time are definitely haunting us, and we are all starting to have sleepless nights.

The signs of the End are; suppose, to make us happy, because the promises of our LORD are now being fulfilled. On this subject I will quote a few chapter's to remind us about what we were told and try to match them with our todays life and the news we read from the newspapers.

I myself am one of the people who are rejoicing to see the signs, because, I am ready to leave earth. And I am ready to move on to see our promised land. I have spoken about this in the begging of this book about the messages which I have received from the LORD about what will happen when we reach the end of time

And everything which the LORD has told me I can see it clearly and it is taking place in the world. And I am pleased that our LORD has never left us in spirit like He told us that He will always be with us.

We will start reading about JOSIAH who is the one the LORD told me that; it will be the spirit of JOSIAH who will come before him to the world, and JOSIAH will prophesy and confirm the end of time to us and also convince those who still do not believe and those who are still practising evil. Josiah is very important to all of us because when he was born the LORD showed him to me but told me that he will only teach us for only two years then he will die at the age of seventeen because his work will only begin at the age of fifteen. At this time he is being looked after by his mother and is well cared for and protected by our LORDS Angels. Josiah is born of flesh in this part of the world but his spirit spends most of the time in Heaven because that is where he belongs, his spirit has taken a new body and a new name. The LORD told me that at this time even Josiah's mother does not realise that he a son who has come change the world by confirming the end of time and convincing those who have given up on GOD.

Since the birth of Josiah I have detached from my body and visited this wonderful baby in about four occasions. He is a cheerful baby and is being looked after very well and his work will commence at the age of fifteen.

PLEASE NOTE

The spirit of JOSIAH has been given the earthly body so that he can be able to communicate with us. And he has been given a new name as well. He will start his work at the age of fifteen years old, and he will preach for only two years and then GOD will take him away from us and then the LORD will come as He promised.

LET US READ ABOUT KING JOSIAH'S PAST LIFE.

2 KINGS 22: 1-2

Josiah was eight when years old when he became King, and he reigned in Jerusalem for thirty one years. His mother's name was Adaiah; she was from BOZKATH. Josiah did what was right in the eyes of the LORD and walked in all the ways of his father David, not turning to the right or the left.

In the eighteenth year of his reign King Josiah sent the secretary Shaphan son of Azaliah, the son of Meshullam, to the temple of the LORD that is the time King Josiah found the <u>book of the laws</u> which was given to him by Hilkiah who was a high Priest.

2KINGS 22:8-

Hilkaiah the high priest said to Stephan the secretary, I have found the book of the law in the temple of the LORD. He gave it to Shaphan, who read it. Then Shaphan the secretary went to the king and reported to him.

2KINGS 22: 10-13

When the king heard the words of the Book of the law, he tore his robes. He gave these orders to Hilkaiah the priest, Ahikam son of Shapan, Acbor son of MIcaiah.

Shapan the secretary and Asaiah the kings attendant; Go and enquire of the LORD for me and for the people and for all Judah about, what is written in this book that has been found?

Great is the LORD'S anger that burns against us, because our fathers have not obeyed the words of this book; they have not acted with all that is written there concerning us.

Hilkiah the priest, Ahikam, Achor, Shapan and Asaiah went to speak to the prophetess Huldah who said to them. The LORD said he will bring disaster on this place and its people, according to everything written in the book the king of Judah has read. Because they have forsaken Him and burnt incense to other gods and provoked Him to anger by all the idols their hands have made. The LORD'S anger will burn against this place and will not be quenched.

2KINGS 23: 1-3

Josiah **R**enews the **C**ovenant.

Then King Josiah called together all the elders of Judah and Jerusalem. He went up to the temple of the LORD with the man of Judah, the people of Jerusalem, the priests and the prophets—all the people from the Least to the Greatest. He read in their hearing all the words of the Book of the Covenant, which had been found in the Temple of the LORD.

The king stood by the pillar and renewed the Covenant in the presence of the LORD—to follow the LORD and keep his Commands, regulations and decrees with all his heart and all his soul, thus confirming the words of the Covenant written in the Book.

Then all the people pledge themselves to the Covenant.

After the people have pledged themselves Josiah started doing the will of GOD and started to demolish all the places which worshipped the gods not the LORD.

Josiah removed from the Temple of the LORD all the articles made for Baal and Asherah and all the starry hosts. He burned them outside Jerusalem in the fields of the Kindron Valley and took the ashes to Bethel.

He did away with the pagan priests appointed by the kings of Judah to burn incense on the high places of the towns of Judah and on those around Jerusalem—those who burned incense in Baal, to the sun and moon, to the constellations and to all the starry hosts.

He took the Asherah Pole from the temple of the LORD to the kindron valley outside Jerusalem and burnt it there. He ground it into powder and scattered the dust over the graves of common people.

He also tore down the quarters of the male shrine-prostitutes, which were in the temple of the LORD and where women did weaving for Asherah.

King Josiah also brought all the priests from the town of Judah and desecrated the high places, from Geba to Beersheba, where the priests have burned incense.

He broke down the shrines at the gates—at the entrance to the gate of Joshua, the city governor, which is on the left of the City Gate. Although the priest of the high places did not serve at the altar of the LORD in Jerusalem, they ate unleavened bread with their fellow priests.

He desecrated Topheth, which was the valley of Ben Hinnom, so no-one could use it to sacrifice his son or daughter in the fire to Molech.

He removed from the entrance to the temple of the LORD the horses of the kings of Judah had dedicated to the sun. They were in the court near the room of an official named Nathen-Melech. Josiah then burned the chariots dedicated to the sun.

He pulled down the altars the kings of Judah had erected on the roof near the upper room of Ahas, and the altars Manasseh had built in the two courts of the temple of the LORD. He removed them from there, smashed them to pieces and threw the rubble into Kidron Valley.

The king also desecrated the high places that were east of Jerusalem on the south of the hill of Corruption—the ones Solomon king of Israel had built for Ashtoreth the vile goddess of the Sidonians, for chemosh the vile god of Moab, and for Molech the detestable god of the people of Ammon. Josiah smashed the sacred stones abd cut down the Asherah poles and covered the sites with human bones.

Even; the Altar at Bethel, the high place made by Jeroboam son of Nebat who had caused Israel to sin, even that Altar and high place he demolished. **H**e burnt the high place and ground it into powder, and burnt the Asherah pole also.

Then Josiah looked around, and when he saw the tombs that were there on the hillside, he had the bones removed from them and burned on the Altar to defile it, in accordance of the word of LORD proclaimed by the man of GOD who foretold these things.

The king Josiah saw the tomb stone and asked; what is that tomb stone I see? The man of the City said; It . . . . marks the tomb of the man of GOD who came from Judah and pronounced against the Altar of Bethel the very things you have done to it.

Then King Josiah said; Leave it alone, "Don't let anyone disturb his bones, So they spared his bones and those of the prophets who have come from Samaria.

Just as he has done at Bethel, King Josiah removed and defiled all the shrines at the high places that the kings of Israel had built in the towns of Samaria that had provoked the LORD to anger.

King Josiah slaughtered all the priests of those high places on the Altars and burned human bones on them. Then he went back to Jerusalem.

Then the KING gave this order to all the people: Celebrate the Passover to the LORD your GOD, as it is written in the BOOK OF THE COVENANT.

Not since the day of the judges who led Israel, nor throughout the days of the kings of Israel and the kings of Judah, had any such Passover been observed. But in the eighteenth year of King Josiah, this Passover was celebrated to the LORD in Jerusalem.

Furthermore King Josiah got rid of; The Mediums, The spiritist's and The household gods!

The Idols and all the other detestable things; seen In Judah and Jerusalem. This he did to fulfil the requirements of the law written in the book that Hilkiah the Priest had discovered in the Temple of the LORD.

Neither Before nor After King Josiah—was there a king like him. Who turned to the LORD as he did!

With all his Heart

AND

119

With all his Soul

AND

With all his Strength!

<u>In accordance with the Law of Moses!</u>

When the LORD asked me to look at the past life of King Josiah, I did not expect to read about such an amazing man who worked so hard to fulfil GOD'S purpose with love. I thought he was coming to teach us and remind us about the teachings in the Bible. Now it makes me wonder if he will do the same like he did in his past life.

<u>JEREMIAH17:7</u>

Blessed is the man who trusts in the LORD; whose confidence is in Him. He will be like a tree planted by the water, that sends out its roots by the stream.

It does not fear when the heat comes; its leaves are always green, it has no worries in a year of drought and never fails to bear fruit.

<u>PLEASE TAKE CARE</u>

The end of the world will always leave us confused because of the messages we have been receiving now and again about the end of the world which will come and destroy everything and those who are good will go to Heaven and those who are bad will go to Hell.

It is true as we know that there is time for everything, because we have seen the seasons change and now we are very good at predicting the weather and all sorts of other things. And we believe whatever people tell us about some things we want to believe. But; when it comes to the end the world, we are still confused.

The prophets of GOD have been preaching these for years about what will happen, now because we can see the truth we do not know what to do and how to prepare ourselves.

The story of King Josiah is the story of Hope and Faith and he teaches us that, we must have faith in GOD and we must believe in GOD because there is GOD who does not pride on evil deeds but punishes those who do not live according to the teachings of Moses.

Now when the LORD asked me to right the story of King Josiah I did not know who he was and what he did, but while I was writing the message from the Bible about his past life I realise, if King Josiah was such a good servant to the LORD in his past life and did all he was ordered to do. This is why the LORD has chosen him to come again this time to come and prepare us.

While I was writing I realised that the changes he did in his past life to the world, were really amazing. And this is what we definitely need at this time, because the people in this world have gone too far doing evil things to others and these evil people seem to be heartless and they hurt so many lives without feeling guilty at all. They are doing exactly what the Prophets tell us not to do.

The truth still states that not everyone is a sinner, we must realise that there are a lot of good people around us but some of these good people are now and again being physically and mentally abused. So they turn to live isolated lives just to keep away from what is going on in the world.

And some of them keep on searching for truth, because they know that GOD is a true GOD and that GOD is love and they share that love with us and encourage us to bring our faith back.

We need to change before the Josiah starts fulfilling GOD'S purpose and we must not wait for GOD to be angry like he did in king Josiah's past life.

We really do not want to experience GOD'S anger again. We all know how we feel when we read about the evil things which are taking place in the world, so why do we think that GOD will rejoice to see such evil? No! GOD does not rejoice in evil deeds. GOD has warned us many times and we are completely ignoring his warnings.

This time is definitely the End of Time.

These are the Law's which our LORD JESUS Christ wants us to keep to. And live according to these laws and if we are still practicing the wrong deed we have to stop. That's it!

I have been asked by the LORD to write these messages to you so that we can all prepare ourselves before His coming, which is soon. And these laws are written in the Bible and the laws which I am asked to quote from the Bible are the very important once which the LORD wants us to keep to and some behaviour which we will need to change as those behaviours are bodily not Spiritual as now is the spiritual time we have to live according to the spiritual needs. The bodily needs are over now. The body was only to house the spirit now we are ready to be transformed to our new bodies. Just as JESUS was transformed we are all ready to be transformed.

Please read about the <u>FOUR STAGES OF THE END OF TIME.</u> This will help you understand that the <u>third stage</u>[3]stage] is the stage of transformation but; to be transformed we need to discard evil deeds. Then after the transformation life on earth will be history to all of us but a purpose to GOD who will transform earth as He wishes. Each individual spirit will evolve to a higher dimension. Because; the purpose of life is to learn, so to be able to evolve!

MATTHEW 17:1-5

After six days JESUS CHRIST took with Him Peter, James and John the brother of James, and led them up a high mountain by themselves. There He was transfigured before them. His face shone like the sun and His clothes became as white as the light.

Just then there appeared before them Moses and Elijah talking with JESUS.

Peter said to JESUS; LORD, it is good for us to be here, if you wish, I will put up three shelters—one for you—one for Moses—one for Elijah.

While he was still speaking, a bright cloud enveloped them and a voice from the cloud said:—This is my son whom I love; with whom I am well pleased, listen to Him.

ECCELESIASTES 7: 27-29

Look," says the teacher; this is what I have discovered:—**A**dding one thing to another to discover the scheme of things, while I was still searching but not finding, I found one upright man among a thousand, but not one upright woman among them all.

This only have I found, **G**OD made mankind upright; **b**ut **m**en have gone in search of many schemes.

PLEASE NOTE

The teacher is right GOD did make man perfect and man created so many things to the point that he forgot who he is and who he was. This is why the Bible and the teaching of all Religions are trying to bring us back to who we were before, because we have lost faith in GOD, and the teachers of Religion are helping us to retrieve our faith in GOD.

WE HAVE LOST OUR FAITH IN GOD

AND

THIS IS WHAT IS HAPPENING IN THE WORLD.

1 CORINTHIANS 2:5

OUR FAITH MUST NOT REST ON MANS WISDOM

BUT

ON GOD'S POWER

THE SOLONIANS 5:24

MAY GOD HIMSELF THE GOD OF PEACE SANTIFY YOU THROUGH AND THROUGH

REVELATIONS 22:17

THE SPIRIT AND THE BRIDE SAY:—COME"

LET HIM WHO HEARS SAY:—COME

WHOEVER IS THIRSTY:—LET HIM COME

WHOEVER WISHES:—LET HIM TAKE THE FREE GIFT OF THE WATER OF LIFE

THE WATER OF LIFE

TO BE ABLE TO DRINK FROM THE SPRING OF THE WATER OF LIFE WE NEED TO BE COMPASSIONATE TO EACH OTHER BEFORE THE END OF THE WORLD CATCHES UP WITH US.

ECCELETIASTES 8: 1

Who is like a wise man?

Who knows the explanation of things?

Wisdom brightens a man's face and changes its hard appearance.

ECCELETIASTES 8: 2-8

SUBMITTING TO THE LORD JESUS CHRIST OUR KING

[1] **O**bey the King's command, I say, because you took an oath before GOD.

[2 **D**o not be in a hurry to leave the king's presence.

[3] **D**o not stand up for a bad cause, for he will do whatever he pleases.

[4] **S**ince a King's word is supreme, who can say to him, **w**hat are you doing?

[5] **W**hoever obeys his command will come to no harm and the wise heart will know the proper time and procedure. **F**OR; **t**here is a proper time and procedure for every matter. **T**hough a man's misery ways weighs heavily upon him! **S**ince no man knows the future, who can tell him what is to come?

No man has power over the wind to contain it.

SO

No—one has power over the day of his death.

SO

No—one is discharged in time of war.

AND

WICKEDNESS WILL NOT RELEASE THOSE WHO PRACTICE IT.

PLEASE TAKE NOTE

Learning the words of wisdom will lead us to righteousness and help us complete the lessons of life gracefully. Words of wisdom are good advice which we get from good people and to be able to understand these words we have to ignore critics and find the truth ourselves and also have to be good listeners and also learn to look for the right answers from different Religious books which will solve some of the missing answers which we are searching for. Do not give up searching it is the only way you will be able to find the truth.

Each Religion has something good to offer us it is you to find-out the truth as no one will find it for you. All Religions come from the same GOD.

Start exploring; this is your life. You were born alone and you will die alone. You were brain washed to believe that your religion is better than the rest. This is what is called oppression. Don't be a victim anymore do your own investigation and live the oppressor confused because the oppressor is confused himself. If he was not confused he would not oppress.

ALL the good Prophets of the past managed to search for the truth and they found it they did not oppress anyone or make themselves feel superior. They were very humble.

Start you journey and evolve.

PROVEBS 29:13

The poor man and the oppressor have this in common: The LORD gives sight to both of them.

WORDS OF WISDOM

Better be a nobody

But

Have wisdom

Wisdom will help us to be able to accept our mistakes and put them right. Stupidity is coursed by refusing to accept our faults. When we do not accept our faults we turn to live in the world of fantasy.

FANTASY

Whoever chases fantasy lacks judgement!

LIPS

Your lips should detest wickedness

ASKING FOR HELP

If you are not sure with about something you are learning:—**Ask**

And

If you still not sure:—**Pray**

THINKING WISELY

Thoughts without actions are meaningless!

EARNING GOOD REWARDS

Doing nothing rewards nothing!

GOOD CHOICES

Better choices bring better rewards

GOOD INTENTIONS

No one cares about what you intend to do!

But

They care only about what you have done!

GOOD BEHAVIOR

Good behaviour brings great rewards!

MAKING YOUR OWN RULES

Make your own rules based on good results!

We have been given dominion over our own lives but we have to make sure that whatever we practice must be righteous. Because; GOD created us to be perfect beings; just like Him.

GOD IS LOVE BEYOND LOVE

The love of GOD to man is beyond believe but man have not acknowledge the presence of GOD in their daily life. And failing to acknowledge the presence of GOD man turned to sin and practised superiority. Now that GOD has taken over the world. Mans superiority has faded away.

SUPERIORITY HAS LOST ITS VOLUME

DO NOT

TRY TO RECOUP IT

OTHERWISE

IT WILL TAKE YOU FOR A FOOL

Superiority is definitely gone now each individual is travelling the lone journey.

The journey of self!

PLEASE NOTE

We can all see what is happening in the world, all the respect which people carried with them some generations back it is all gone. We are left with the observation of the world which is coming to the end.

We must listen to the wise man of GOD who will teach us how to prepare ourselves.

THE TONGUE OF THE WISEMAN

BRINGS

HEALING TRUTH

The LORD has now prepared the wise man who, will come and prepare us and we should listen to him when he comes because he is coming to change every nation from the four corners of the world to prepare them for the coming of the LORD.

The LORD has also prepared eighteen spiritual books which should be read when they are released, some of these books are already in the market and people are already learning from these books.

Some books will come as fictional books but what is written will not be fiction it will be reality in disguise.

Some of the books will be based on mysteries, visions and messages received by the authors. And we must search for the truth because the truth is revealing itself in many forms.

We must become good servants of the LORD just like King Josiah who fulfilled GODS purpose with loyalty. The leaders of today must be loyal to their people so to help them travel this wonderful journey with love. And that will help the leaders to be able to travel their journey with love.

LOYALTY TO ALL

PROVEBS 29: 14

If a king judges the poor with fairness, his throne will always be secure.

King Josiah was the king amongst kings

2 KINGS 23: 28-30

As for the other events of King Josiah's reign, and all he did, are written in the book of Annals of the King of Judah.

While Josiah was king, Pharaoh Neco king of Egypt went up to the Eupharates River to help the king of Assyria. King Josiah marched out to meet him in battle, but Neco faced him and killed him at Megiddo.

Josiah's servants brought his body in a chariot from Megiddo to Jerusalem and buried him in his own tomb. King Josiah fulfilled his purpose with Love

How about you?

PLEASE TAKE NOTE

We must have trust in the LORD. This is what John The Baptist says to us.

JOHN 21:25

JESUS DID MANY OTHER THINGS AS WELL

IF

EVERY ONE OF THEM WERE WRITTEN DOWN I SUPPOSE THAT EVEN THE WHOLE WORLD—WOULD NOT HAVE ROOM FOR THE BOOKS WHICH WOULD HAVE BEEN WRITTEN.

PRAISE BE TO OUR LORD JESUS CHRIST

LET US CARRYON LEARNING THE WORDS OF WISDOM FROM THE PROPHETS OF GOD. AS WE CAN ALL SEE THAT THE WORLD HAS TURNED AGAINST US AND WE ARE NOW GOING THROUGH PAINFUL TESTS AND PUNISHMENT! SOME OF US ARE PUNISHING THEMSELVES BY USING SUBSTANCES WHICH KILL THE BODY AND SOME OF US ARE BEING PUNISHED BY OTHERS.

PROVEBS 17: 26

It is not good to punish an innocent man.

This is what the world is doing today! They are punishing innocent people, because they are cowards, they are afraid to face the oppressor. And the oppressor carries on with his dirty deals.

LET US NOW LEARN ABOUT THINGS WHICH DELAY OUR SPIRITUAL GROWTH

ALCOHOL AND DRUGS

PROVEBS 23: 19-21

Listen, my son, be wise, and keep your heart on the right path.

Do not join those who drink too much wine or gorge themselves on meat. For drunkards and gluttons become poor. And drowsiness clothes them in rags.

RESPECT FOR PARENTS

PROVEBS 23:22-25

Listen to your father, who gave you—life.

AND

Do not despise your mother when she is old.

Buy the truth and do not sell it;

Get wisdom, Discipline and understanding.

PROSTITUTE'S MUST STOP THIS EVILNESS

PROVEBS 23:27-28

For a prostitute is—a deep pit and a wayward wife is a narrow well; like a bandit she lies in wait, and multiplies the unfaithful among men, who has woe, who has sorrow, who has strife, who has complaints, who has needless bruises, who has bloodshot eyes.

AND

Those; who linger over wine, who go and sample bowls of mixed wine.

WINE AND [ALCOHOL OF ANY KIND]
AND
DRUGS WHICH ARE USED TODAY

PROVEBS 23: 31-35

Do not gaze at wine when it is red, when it sparkles in the cup, when it goes down smoothly! In the end it bites like a snake and poison like a viper.

Your eyes will see strange sights and your mind imagine confusing things. You will be like one sleeping on the high seas, lying on top of the rigging.

They hit me—you will say; but—I am not hurt!

They beat me—you will say; but—I don't feel it!

When

Will I wake up and find another drink.

PLEASE NOTE

These days we have a problem with drug addiction which is the same as alcohol, people needing what they call a fix every hour, because they have damaged their bodies and their brains and they can't think straight anymore and they live in a world of pain.

This is what the Bible is teaching us about:—To be careful with all the intoxicants, because they damage our brains and destroy lives and that leads to losing the purpose of our journey. When we stop these intoxicants we will be able to use our wisdom.

PROVEBS 2: 12-15

Wisdom will save you from the ways of the wicked men, from men;—whose words are perverse.

Men who leave the straight paths, to walk in dark ways!

Men who delight in doing wrong and rejoice in the perverseness of Evil!

Men whose paths are crooked and who are devious in their ways!

PROVERBS 2: 16-22

Wisdom will save you from the adulteress, from the wayward wife with her seductive words, who has left the partner of her youth.

AND

Ignored the covenant she made before GOD

For

Her house leads down to death!

And

Her path to the spirits of the dead!

None

Who go to her!

Return or attain the paths of life!

PROVERBS 2: 20-22

Therefore walk in the ways of good men and keep and to the paths of the righteous.

FOR

The upright will live in the land, and the blameless will remain in it.

BUT

The wicked will be cut off from the land!

AND

The unfaithful will be torn from it!

ISAIAH 45: 22

TURN TO ME AND BE SAVED ALL YOU END'S OF THE EARTH

FOR:—I AM GOD AND THERE IS NO OTHER!

ACTS 17:26-28

GOD gives all men life and breath and everything else!

From; One man he made every nation of men, that they should inhabit the whole earth.

And determined the times set for them and the exact places where they should live.

GOD; did this so that men would seek Him and perhaps, reach out for Him and find Him! Though! He is not far from each one of us!

For in Him we live and move and have our being!

As

Some of your poets have said we are His offspring.

ACTS 18: 9-10

DO NOT BE AFRAID KEEP ON SPEAKING

DO NOT BE SILENT FOR I AM WITH YOU!

<u>Daniel 6: 21-22</u>

Daniel answered, "O king, live for ever! MY GOD sent his Angel and shut the mouths of the lions.

They have not hurt me, because I was found innocent in his sight. Nor have I ever done any wrong before you, O king.

I can't imagine how the king felt. He must have felt so embarrassed. I bet he did wet his pants a bit. That's what I call—Defeated. Well done Daniel good for you.

<u>REVELATIONS 22: 7-10</u>

<u>JESUS IS COMING SOON</u>

Behold, I am coming soon! Blessed is he who keeps the words of the prophets in this book.

I John am the one who heard and saw these things. And when I had heard and seen them, I fell down to worship at the feet of the Angel who had been showing them to me. But, he said to me. Do not do it! I am a fellow-servant with you and with your brothers the prophets and of all who keep the words of this book.

Worship GOD.

<u>PLEASE TAKE NOTE</u>

I hope you are enjoying the reading in this book and the messages from the LORD. The TEACHINGS FROM THE PROPHETS about things which delay are spiritual. These are things which we should discard in our lives they were only the lessons of life now it is time for the lessons of the spirit. We all know and have seen how dangerous substances can harm our bodies and how prostitutes have destroyed loving families and what happens to alcoholics. All this kind of behaviour is sin to the body. This is why the LORD asked me to warn those who are still practicing this kind of behaviour to stop so that they can now turn to GOD for the forgiveness of sins, because the LORD is coming soon.

We do not need to do evil things to keep ourselves joyful. life is really beautiful when we see it with undamaged minds.

THIS IS HOW I SEE LIFE

I see life as—a never ending Dream.

I see life as—a mirror of me.

I see life as—an expression of self!

I see life as a never ending mystery of GOD'S Creation.

HOW
DO YOU SEE LIFE?

THE JOURNEY OF LIFE IS THE JOURNEY OF SELF

Introduction.... Baby Josiah.... Year.... Year.... Year.... Reading from John .... The seven thousand years .... Transformation.... The day of rapture .... Year .... The seven levels of our spiritual growth .... Reading from the Bible .... Words of wisdom .... Nothing changes .... Physical Abuse and Mental Abuse .... For the love of money .... Remember your creator .... For those who love GOD .... Forgiveness is what we are left with .... Do not be afraid .... Devil released .... Devil chained .... Josiah .... Words of wisdom .... Smile .... What is forgiveness .... Words of wisdom .... The world .... The ways of the LORD .... Prayer .... Loneliness .... Words of wisdom .... Knowledge .... To, overcome fear .... Thinking .... What is evil .... Act of love .... GOD'S WILL .... Forgiveness .... Perfection .... Boasting .... Religions .... Faith .... GOD is love .... The light .... Do not be afraid .... God is spirit .... Words of wisdom .... Humanity ... Sharing our gifts .... Temptation .... Favouritism .... Love .... How to overcome evil .... Happiness .... Living a quiet life .... Message of comfort .... Temptations .... Humbleness .... This awesome world .... JESUS heals a blind man .... The delayed book of laws .... Introduction .... Message of love .... Blind man fulfilled his purpose .... Learning our lessons .... How much do we know.... Think carefully.... We are not responsible for other failures .... Reading from John .... The Ten Commandments .... Message I received ... Other messages .... Spiritual gifts .... The world and message of hope .... A time to plant and time to uproot.... Our Leaders .... Message to our Leaders .... Message of comfort.... A time to kill and time to heal .... A time to tear down and a time to build .... You shall not murder .... A time to weep and a time to laugh .... A time to mourn and a time to dance .... The rest of the times ... Words of wisdom .... The prayer .... Message to all .... The signs of the end .... King

Josiah . . . . Message to all . . . . The signs of the end . . . Words of wisdom . . . . What do we need to change . . . . King Josiah's death . . . . We must trust in GOD . . . . Words of wisdom . . . . Alcohol and drugs . . . . Wisdom . . . . Do not be afraid . . . . How do I see life . . . .

THANK YOU LORD.

CHAPTER SEVEN [7]

Chapter seven is an update of messages received after the book was almost ready to be published. I received these messages while I was writing the book called THE COMPOSED JOURNEY OF THE SPIRIT. This book is based on the teaching of the LORD by using diagrams in one of the messages in this book is the message of the four stages of the end of time which I have added earlier in this book.

The four stages of the end of time seems to almost coordinate with the day of the rapture which was predicted by the peoples radio station, when they told us that the rapture will arise in the year 2011 on the month of May on the fifth day.

UPDATE

Yes it is now on the twenty fourth of May the year twenty eleven [24/5/2011] and the leaflet which I have received in Cape Town about the Rapture which was to occur in the world on the [21/5/2011].

Yes!

The rapture did happen; as quite of a few chosen children of GOD were anointed and the LORD directed me to confirm to this people that they were anointed with light of GOD. Every person I spoke to—told me that they felt very happy and they knew that something in their lives has changed but, they did not know what it was. They only felt love within them. It gave me so much pleasure to be able to meet these chosen children of GOD. People were spiritually anointed on the day of the [21/5'2011]***** But, not taken away yet. The rapture only means that GOD has started to anoint His chosen people and this has now taken place and it will carry on until the end of time.

The Family radio station which told us about the rapture were not trying to hurt us they are actually helping us to be prepared for the end of time, unfortunately some people saw this opportunity as a time to take advantage of others and to hurt people because they thought it will be the end of time and they can do whatever pleases them.

The end of time messages which we have been hearing now and again will only happen at the time which GOD has chosen just as the LORD told us. And it only means that we should re-look at our lives and change the things which needs changing and to live a good life without doing evil, because we know that evil deeds only end us into fear and depression and also end us in prison.

Life will carry on as it has been; but the spiritual changes will be taking place daily in our lives until the end of time. And a lot of people will be fulfilling their purposes and finishing learning their lessons of life and will be directed by GOD our Father because now it is GOD'S time and He has taken over the ruling of the world.

So we must embrace these messages and try to understand what we are being told, the messages did not tell us to do evil deeds it only told us to prepare ourselves.

I myself did use this opportunity to listen to the voice of GOD and to fulfil GOD'S purpose by listening to what GOD instructed me to write and what to tell the world. I did not stop writing the messages I received. What I did was to carry-on with my work because I knew that if GOD wants me to write I will write, whether is the end or no end. I will carry on doing my duty to GOD.

GOD did direct me to meet the anointed people and it was a great pleasure to give these wonderful people their messages and in most of these cases GOD made sure that I give these messages in front of people who knew these individuals so that there can be a testimony.

Yes it is true I have met these people which GOD anointed on the same-day when a lot of people believed that the end of the time has come. Our LORD told me that it was the day of the beginning of our anointment and the thesaurus tells us clearly that Rapture means:—Joy, Bliss, Delight, Euphoria, Enthusiasm, and it even mentions the Heavenly feeling.

Yes when I gave these messages there was so much joy and we were all experiencing the Heavenly feeling on earth and it was wonderful.

PLEASE TAKE NOTE

The people whom GOD OUR FATHER anointed on that day; these are the people I have no Idea about their life style and these are the people I did not know but, I was sent to them and some people approached me and told me that I have a message for them, then immediately GOD will start giving this wonderful message to tell them that they were anointed on that day.

The messages of the end of time are meant to strengthen our faith in GOD not to lead us to practising evil deeds. We have to thank the FAMILY RADIO STATION for bringing us closer to GOD our Creator.

ISAIAH 46:8-13

REMEMBER, THIS; FIX IT IN MIND; TAKE IT TO HEART, YOU REBELS. REMEMBER THE FORMER THINGS THOSE OF LONG AGO.

I AM GOD AND THERE IS NO OTHER!

I AM GOD AND THERE IS NONE LIKE ME!

I MAKE KNOWN THE END FROM THE BEGINNING.

FROM

ANCIENT TIMES WHAT IS IT TO COME!

I SAY; MY PURPOSE WILL STAND.

AND

I WILL DO ALL THAT I PLEASE.

FROM THE EAST I WILL SUMMON A BIRD OF PRAY.

FROM A FAR-OFF LAND

A MAN TO FULFIL MY PURPOSE!

WHAT I HAVE SAID:—THAT I WILL BRING.

WHAT I HAVE PLANNED:—THAT WILL I DO.

LISTEN TO ME

YOU STUBBORN-HEARTED—YOU ARE FAR FROM RIGHTEOUSNESS!

I AM BRINGING MY RIGHTEOUSNESS NEAR!

IT IS NOT FAR AWAY AND MY SALVATION WILL NOT BE DELAYED.

I WILL GRANT SALVATION TO ZION AND MY SPLENDOUR TO ISRAEL!

PLEASE TAKE NOTE

ZION means all the worshipers of GOD who are all over the world and are worshiping GOD in different Religions.

ISRAEL means the spirit of GOD which dwells inside all of us.

THANKS BE TO GOD OUR FATHER

LIFE IS ALL ABOUT GENERATING LOVE!